*Civil Rights During the Kennedy Administration*

President John F. Kennedy at news conference in the State Department Auditorium, Nov. 14, 1963.

—World Wide Photos

The UNIVERSITY & COLLEGE PRESS OF MISSISSIPPI is a non-profit endeavor for the publishing of scholarly books from Alcorn A & M College, Delta State College, Jackson State College, Mississippi State College for Women, Mississippi State University, Mississippi Valley State College, University of Southern Mississippi and the University of Mississippi and others.

UNIVERSITY & COLLEGE PRESS OF MISSISSIPPI
SOUTHERN STATION, BOX 5164
HATTIESBURG, MISS. 39401

*To my wife, Dr. Maria Luisa Alvarez Harvey and son, Roger*

# Foreword

When, finally, the glamour and the romance of Camelot fade, the Kennedy years are likely still to be remembered as an era in which the country's energies and concerns were brought into focus on the social ills affecting the South—most notably in the denial of civil rights to Negroes. Yet, as Professor Harvey points out, the young president fell short of bringing about a legislative program of reform which, as his administration progressed, was seen to be so palpably needed.

Kennedy critics have charged that it was only under the pressure of increasing civil rights demonstrations that the president responded in a positive way to the demands of the times. There are many who felt that, at the beginning of his term, he was not fully committed to the civil rights cause, and there are those who charge that his eloquence when he did become committed contributed to the rising expectations of black Americans which, given the reality of the South and, indeed, of the nation could not immediately be translated into visible change in the lives of people.

Both charges could well be subjects of scholarly works in themselves. They are dealt with briefly and pointedly here. Of the former Mr. Harvey takes the pragmatic view that Kennedy's "being passionate or not is not so important as what he actually did while in office." Of the latter he freely admits that "the president promised more than he could deliver in such a few years."

What the president did achieve, as it emerges in Mr. Harvey's book, was to create a political atmosphere in which social change could take place, relying on executive action, example, power and prestige, and his own personal popularity with the people.

Mr. Harvey's book is essentially a record from the outside,

drawn for the most part from documents of the period. It is a valuable record as a study of executive leadership in crisis, and as such it draws a sharp, if implicit, contrast between a leadership of a decade ago and leadership which guides the country today.

Robert E. Anderson, Jr.

Editor, Southern Regional Council Publications
February 1971

# Preface

The purpose of this study is to analyze and evaluate the actions taken by the Kennedy Administration in the area of Civil Rights. More specifically the emphasis is on John Kennedy's use of the different levers available to the chief executive in dealing with problems of racial discrimination.

In terms of methodology the approach is descriptive and analytical. In Chapter 1 the major accomplishments of the Roosevelt, Truman, and Eisenhower administrations in the field of civil rights are reviewed. Chapter 2 contains a discussion of the 1960 presidential campaign and the role played by the civil rights issue in its tenor and outcome. Following the victory of John F. Kennedy, there is an explanation of the obstacles he faced and the tools he had at his command by which to assault discriminatory practices. Finally, there is a brief discussion of the strategy he decided to adopt in promoting civil rights. Chapter 3 is an analysis and description of President John F. Kennedy's attack on discrimination in the following areas: appointment to high governmental posts, attendance at social as well as official functions by governmental officials, housing, the armed forces, transportation, education, and employment. There is a focus on the levers which the president used to expand the available opportunities for black Americans. Chapter 4 contains a partial case study of the drive for a civil rights bill in 1963. The president of course, died before he could complete his task. In the epilogue, an overview is made of Kennedy's accomplishments in civil rights together with a discussion of the tools of executive power he used, and a general comparison between his actions and of his three predecessors.

I do not pretend that this is an exhaustive study of the subject dealt with in the manuscript. I hope that those who read it will be encouraged to delve more deeply into this most important domestic problem for our society.

In preparing this manuscript I received invaluable guidance and assistance from Dr. Clifford Lytle, Head of the Department of Government at The University of Arizona. In addition, I would like to thank Jackson State College and the University & College Press of Mississippi for making this publication possible. Finally, I am grateful to Mr. Robert E. Anderson, Jr., Editor of the Southern Regional Council Publications, Atlanta, Georgia, for writing the introduction.

James C. Harvey
March, 1971

# Contents

# 1. Background: Recent Presidents and Civil Rights

Some seven decades after being "freed," black Americans found themselves hampered by all kinds of racial restrictions and at the bottom of the economic and social ladder in the United States. Dramatic changes, however, were to occur along with the development of the modern presidency.

Precedents for action in the civil rights field undertaken by the Kennedy Administration had been actually initiated during the administrations of Roosevelt, Truman, and Eisenhower. During the New Deal President Roosevelt instituted innovative social and economic programs which, while not directly related to civil rights, were nevertheless beneficial to low income groups among whom Negroes were the most conspicuous. In spite of the gains, however, few Negroes were able to penetrate the segregated institutions in American society. The bread lines and the soup kitchens were frequently operated on a segregated basis. Indeed, even the employment services provided for segregation during the depression.

Despite the lack of progress in dealing with racial barriers, there was an administrative change made in 1939 that was important for the future. In that year, Attorney General Frank Murphy created a Civil Liberties Section—subsequently called the Civil Rights Section—in the Criminal Division of the Department of Justice.

As World War II approached, Negro leaders sensed how hypocritical it was to claim that Americans were democratic and opposed to totalitarianism while blacks were all but excluded from the privileges in American society. They dramatized their cause by demanding an end to discrimination in employment in defense industries. By threatening a march on Washington they forced the

1

president to issue an executive order prohibiting such discrimination and establishing a Fair Employment Practices Committee to enforce the policy.¹ Segregation continued in the armed forces during the war, but toward the end of hostilities an experiment was undertaken to place Negroes and whites in the same fighting units.

Roosevelt's successor, Harry Truman, was unable to preserve the FEPC and it was abolished by congressional action shortly after the war. In seeking to preserve some type of governmental mechanism, the president created a more limited body, the Committee on Government Contract Compliance. This agency was given the responsibility of promoting equal employment opportunity among those firms engaged in business transactions with the federal government. In addition, he appointed the President's Commission on Civil Rights and adopted as his own its then bold recommendations which called for anti-lynching, anti-poll tax, and fair employment laws. In fact, Truman waged an aggressive campaign for the enactment of these proposals by Congress. Although his legislative efforts failed, he demonstrated in 1948 that a Democrat could be elected president without the support of the segregationist elements in the South, and he set a precedent for legislative proposals that would become law under later administrations. Finally, in perhaps his most far-reaching act in civil rights, Truman issued an executive order in 1948 dealing with the elimination of segregation in the armed forces.²

In the meantime the United States Supreme Court handed down a series of decisions validating the Negroes' constitutional claims to equality under the law. It upheld the rights of Negroes to travel unsegregated on interstate carriers in *Morgan* v. *Virginia* (325 U.S. 373, 1946) during the Truman Administration; to register and vote in southern Democratic primaries in *Nixon* v. *Herndon* (273 U.S. 536, 1927), *Nixon* v. *Condon* (286 U.S. 73, 1932), *Smith* v. *Allwright* (321 U.S. 649, 1944), and *Terry* v. *Adams* (345 U.S. 461, 1953) during the Coolidge, Hoover, Roosevelt, and Eisenhower administrations respectively; and to matriculate in publicly supported institutions of higher learning under certain conditions in *Missouri ex. rel. Gaines* v. *Canada* (305 U.S. 337, 1938), *Sweatt* v. *Painter* (339 U.S. 629, 1950), and *McLaurin* v.

*Oklahoma State Regents* (339 U.S. 637, 1950) during the Roosevelt and Truman administrations. The climax of this judicial revolution came in 1954 when the court repudiated the "separate but equal" doctrine and ruled that racially segregated public schools were unconstitutional, in *Brown* v. *Board of Education* (347 U.S. 483, 1954). This decision left no doubt that ultimately all forms of publicly supported segregation would be prohibited.

The urgency of civil rights for Negroes had been mounting steadily since 1945, and the school desegregation cases pushed the problem to the forefront of our domestic concerns. While blacks were becoming increasingly militant in their demands for equal rights, white southerners became increasingly resistant to racial changes. At this stage the blacks could count on a great deal of white liberal support outside the South.

It was ironic that at the time when the historic *Brown* decision was made and the racial crisis was coming to the forefront, the presidency was assumed by a man whose personal and political philosophy was antipathetic to strong leadership. Throughout his eight years in the White House President Eisenhower reiterated his essentially laissez-faire views on civil rights.[3] He believed that the problem could be resolved most effectively at the local level and at an evolutionary pace, that laws dealing with civil rights were of dubious value, that alteration of the "hearts and minds of men" was a prerequisite for change, and that intervention by the federal government in local affairs was to be assiduously avoided.[4] He even refused to throw the moral weight of his office into the balance, repeatedly declining to express his personal view of the *Brown* decision.

Later President Eisenhower discussed this matter in his memoirs.

> After the Supreme Court's 1954 ruling, I refused to say whether I approved or disapproved of it. The court's judgment was law, I said, and I would abide by it. This determination was one of principle. I believed that if I should express publicly, either approval or disapproval of a Supreme Court decision in one case, I would be obligated to do so in many, if not all, cases. I would eventually be drawn into a public statement of disagreement with some decisions

creating a suspicion that my vigor of enforcement would, in such cases, be in doubt. Moreover, to indulge in a practice of approving or criticizing court decisions could tend to lower the dignity of the government, and would in the long run, be hurtful. In this case, I definitely agreed with the unanimous decision.[5]

For many white liberals and blacks the president's failure to express his approval seemed intolerable. Some of them even felt that his silence indicated at least a lack of concern and encouraged segregationist opposition to the *Brown* decision. As one writer pointed out:

Mr. Eisenhower seemed not to comprehend that Brown v. Board of Education was not just any Supreme Court decision but was one in which the Supreme Court reaffirmed one of the fundamental tenets of the American creed, equality before the law. In refusing to express his personal opinion on such a vital matter, Mr. Eisenhower created the impression, presumably unintentionally, that he did not agree with the principle of equal protection of the laws.[6]

Nevertheless, in spite of the low priority accorded civil rights by the president, some noteworthy executive actions were taken. The Contract Compliance Committee established by Truman was continued under the chairmanship of Vice President Nixon. Unfortunately the committee relied largely on broad programs of public relations and did little to improve the economic status of the Negro.[7] President Eisenhower created another committee to increase equal employment opportunity within the federal civil service. Moreover, the president appointed a Negro, E. Frederick Morrow, to the White House staff, and another, J. Ernest Wilkins, became the assistant secretary of labor.

In addition, Eisenhower carried forward the integration of the armed services. He exercised effective leadership in the desegregation of public accommodations and schools in the nation's capital. Even though his personal role was ambiguous, his administration, at the instigation of Attorneys General Brownell and Rogers, proposed the first successful civil rights legislation since Reconstruction—the Civil Rights Acts of 1957 and 1960, both of which dealt primarily with voting rights. For the first time a

Civil Rights Division was established within the Justice Department under authority granted by the act of 1957. Moreover, the Civil Rights Commission was created as a result of the same act. Eisenhower's most important civil rights action was his dispatch of federal troops to Little Rock in September 1957. The attempt of Arkansas Governor Orval Faubus to thwart a federal court decree which called for the admission of nine Negro pupils to Little Rock High School and the rioting that followed posed a supreme test as to the enforceability of federal court orders. President Eisenhower, reversing his earlier indecision, took decisive action by federalizing ten-thousand members of the Arkansas National Guard and by dispatching one-thousand men of the 101st Airborne Division to Little Rock. However reluctant, President Eisenhower set an irrevocable precedent for the use of military power when it was found necessary to quell active resistance to federal court orders.

It thus is clear that several important preliminary steps were taken by Presidents Roosevelt, Truman, and Eisenhower to alleviate the conditions of the blacks and bring them into the real citizenship class in the United States. However, in view of the magnitude of the problem, the surface had scarcely been scratched. As the 1960 presidential campaign approached, the blacks looked for far stronger leadership from the presidency and for more federal governmental actions at every level to improve their lot.

# 2. JFK, the 1960 Election, and Its Immediate Aftermath

By 1960 not only did the racial issue become increasingly a matter of vital national concern, but it was destined to be placed high on the next administration's agenda. In order to discover what each major political party and its leadership had in mind with regard to a civil rights program, let us examine the platforms, acceptance speeches, and the election campaign itself. Moreover, I will analyze the immediate aftermath of the election as far as civil rights were concerned.

Early in 1960 the effort to awaken the American public to its racial problems began a new phase. Four black college students at Greensboro, North Carolina, entered a variety store, made a few purchases, and afterwards sat down at the lunch counter to order coffee. Although they were refused service, the students remained in their seats until the lunch counter was closed. Out of this event emerged a new form of persuasion the Negro could utilize—the sit-in. The sit-in movement caught on quickly and took place in variety, drug, and department stores with the idea of ending discrimination in their services. The sit-ins occurred in many parts of the country, including Nashville, New Orleans, Chattanooga, Memphis, and Atlanta. This new method of protest was widely publicized by the mass media, and the whites became increasingly aware of the indignities suffered by the blacks.[1] In turn this increased awareness of the black's condition had an impact on politics, as was revealed at both national party conventions in 1960.

The Democrats held their convention first, and in addition to nominating Senator John F. Kennedy of Massachusetts for president and Senator Lyndon B. Johnson of Texas for vice president, they adopted the most far-reaching civil rights stand of any major political party in American history. Chester Bowles was the chairman of the Platform Committee, and he worked closely with Harris L. Wofford, Jr., who was the civil rights specialist on Senator Kennedy's staff. Bowles drafted language which incorporated virtually all the legislative proposals that had been offered for consideration by the civil rights advocates on Capitol Hill.

Among other things, the Democrats in their platform declared that:

What is now required is effective political and moral leadership by the whole executive branch of our government to make equal opportunity a living reality for all Americans.

As the party of Jefferson, we shall provide that leadership.

In every city and state in greater or lesser degree there is discrimination based on color, race, religion, or national origin.

If discrimination in voting, education, the administration of justice or segregated lunch-counters are the issues in one area, discrimination in housing and employment may be pressing questions elsewhere.

The peaceful demonstrations for first class citizenship which have recently taken place in many parts of the country are a signal to all of us to make good at long last the guarantees of our Constitution.

The time has come to assure equal access for all Americans in all areas of community life, including voting booths, schoolrooms, jobs, housing and public facilities.

In specific areas the Democrats made the following pledges:

*Voting:*

The Democratic administration which takes office next January will therefore use the full powers provided in the Civil Rights Acts of 1957 and 1960 to secure for all Americans the right to vote.

If these powers, vigorously invoked by a new Attorney General and backed by a strong and imaginative Democratic President, prove inadequate, further powers will be sought.

We will support whatever action is necessary to eliminate

literacy tests and the payment of poll taxes as requirements for voting.

## Public Schools:

A new Democratic administration will also use its full powers—legal and moral—to insure the beginning of good faith compliance with the constitutional requirements that racial discrimination be ended in public education.

We believe that every school district affected by the Supreme Court's school desegregation decision should submit a plan providing for at least first-step compliance by 1963, the one hundredth anniversary of the Emancipation Proclamation.

To facilitate compliance, technical and financial assistance should be given school districts facing special problems of transition.

For this and for the protection of all other constitutional rights of Americans, the Attorney General should be empowered and directed to file civil injunction suits in federal courts to prevent the denial of any civil rights on grounds of race, color, or creed.

## Employment:

The new Democratic administration will support federal legislation establishing a fair employment practices commission effectively to secure for everyone the right to equal opportunity for employment.

In 1949 the President's Committee on Civil Rights recommended a permanent commission on civil rights. A new Democratic administration will broaden the scope and strengthen the powers of the present commission and make it permanent.

In addition, the Democratic administration will use its full executive powers to assure equal employment opportunities and to terminate racial segregation throughout federal services and institutions, and on all government contracts. The successful desegregation of the armed forces took place through such decisive executive action under President Truman.

*Housing:*

Similarly the new Democratic administration will take action to end discrimination in federal housing programs, including federally assisted housing.

Toward the end the Democrats stated that to "accomplish these goals will require executive orders, legal actions brought by the Attorney General, legislation and improved Congressional procedures to safeguard majority rule."[2] The reference to majority rule obviously meant that Senate Rule 22 and cloture should be changed.

In his acceptance speech at the convention John Kennedy thanked the delegates for nominating him and declared: "I am grateful, too, that you have provided me with such an eloquent statement of our Party's Platform Pledges which so eloquently made are to be kept. "The Rights of Man"—the civil and economic rights essential to the human dignity of all men—are indeed our goal and our first principles. This is a platform on which I can run with enthusiasm and conviction."[3]

Later, in the same speech, Kennedy alluded to the need for changes on the domestic front in order to cope with the current problems. In an attack on the Eisenhower administration he declared that "A peaceful revolution for human rights—demanding an end to racial discrimination in all parts of our community life has strained at the leashes imposed by timid executive leadership."[4] He made it plain that, if elected, he would provide leadership to deal with discrimination against the Negro.

The Republicans held their national convention two weeks later and nominated Vice President Richard Nixon for president and Henry Cabot Lodge, ambassador to the United Nations, for vice president. It appeared that the Republican platform committee, operating under the chairmanship of Charles Percy, would take a conservative stand on civil rights. Although Percy was considered a liberal, the committee had a strong conservative bent since each state had two representatives on it. This meant that the South was in a position to make its position felt.

While the committee worked on the draft, Governor Nelson Rockefeller became increasingly perplexed by what he heard. He and his lieutenants threatened a floor fight over the platform unless a more liberal stand on civil rights was taken. Richard Nixon, the front runner for the nomination at the time, wanted a harmonious convention; and, moreover, he was apprehensive since Rockefeller was regarded as a contender for the presidential nomination.

In order to ward off the threat to unity and to pacify Rockefeller and his supporters, Nixon requested a meeting with the New York governor. It was held in New York. As a result a compact was made in which Nixon agreed to many of Rockefeller's views, including those on civil rights.[5] Over the objections of many of its members Nixon then persuaded the platform committee to modify its earlier civil rights stand and adopt those of the Nixon-Rockefeller compact. Soon thereafter Rockefeller dropped out of contention for the nomination.

In their platform the Republicans, as expected, praised the actions taken by the Eisenhower administration in the field of civil rights. They also endorsed the Supreme Court's decisions in the school desegregation cases.

In specific areas, the Republicans pledged themselves as follows:

*Voting:*

Continued vigorous enforcement of the civil rights laws to guarantee the right to vote to all citizens in all parts of the country; and Legislation to provide that the completion of six primary grades in a state accredited school is conclusive evidence of literacy for voting purposes.

*Public Schools:*

The Department of Justice will continue its vigorous support of court orders for desegregation. Desegregation suits now pending involve at least 39 school districts. Those suits and others already included will affect most major cities in which school desegregation is being practiced.

We will propose legislation to authorize the Attorney General to bring actions for school desegregation in the name of the United States in appropriate cases, as when economic coercion or threat of physical harm is used to deter persons from going to court to establish their rights.

It will use the new authority provided by the Civil Rights Act of 1960 to prevent obstruction of court orders.

Our continued support of the President's proposal to extend federal aid and technical assistance to schools which in good faith attempt to desegregate.

We oppose the pretense of fixing a target date three years from now for the mere submission of plans for desegregation. School districts could construe it as a three-year moratorium during which progress would cease, postponing until 1963 the legal process to enforce compliance. We believe that each of the pending court actions should proceed as the Supreme Court has directed and that in no district should there be any such delay.

*Employment:*

Continued support for legislation to establish a commission on equal job opportunity to make permanent and to expand with legislative backing the excellent work being performed by the President's Committee on Government Contracts.

Use of full-scale review of existing state laws and of prior proposals for federal legislation to eliminate discrimination in employment now being conducted by the Civil Rights Commission for guidance in our objective of developing a federal-state program in the employment area; and special consideration of training programs aimed at developing the skills of those now working in marginal agricultural employment in industry, notably in the new industries moving into the South.

*Housing:*

Action to prohibit discrimination in housing constructed with the aid of federal subsidies.

*Public Facilities:*

Removal of any vestige of discrimination in the operation of federal facilities or procedures which may at any time be found; Opposition to the use of federal funds for the construction of segregated community facilities; Action to ensure that public transportation and other Government authorized services shall be free of segregation.

*Legislative Procedure:*

Our best efforts to change present Rule 22 of the Senate and other appropriate Congressional procedures that often make unattainable proper legislative implementation of Constitutional guarantees.

Toward the end, in obvious reference to the sit-ins, the Republicans declared: "We affirm the Constitutional right to peaceable assembly to protest discrimination in private business establishments."[6]

In his accepting the nomination, Nixon spoke of building a better America and declared that "for the millions of Americans who are still denied equality of rights and opportunity, I say there shall be the greatest progress in human rights since the days of Lincoln a hundred years ago."[7] Later in the address he discussed the need for a strengthening of America in face of the threat posed by communism. In order to accomplish this goal he insisted that:

". . . it means on the part of each American assuming responsibility to make this country which we love, a proud example, doing our part in ending this prejudice which, 100 years after Lincoln, to our shame, still embarrasses us abroad and saps our strength at home."[8]

Shortly after the Republican National Convention was held, President Eisenhower called Congress into special session and requested the adoption of a legislative program, including a civil rights measure. In this request he called for the creation of a permanent President's Commission on Equal Job Opportunity and for federal financial assistance to areas desegregating their schools. Although a bill embodying these programs was introduced in the Senate, it was tabled by a vote of 54 to 28.[9] No action was taken in the House. The Democratic senators charged that the Republicans were engaging in a political maneuver and that there was not enough time to consider the bill since the election campaign was already under way.

Following the failure of the administration's civil rights bill in the Senate, Senator Kennedy and twenty-three other Democratic senators issued a statement condemning the Republican civil rights record. They charged that the Eisenhower administration had carefully avoided opportunities for executive action in civil rights. They pointed out, for example, that the president had not issued a housing order as he could have done by a "stroke of his pen." Their declaration concluded: "We pledge action to obtain consideration of a civil rights bill by the Senate early next session that will implement the pledges of the Democratic platform."[10]

John Kennedy took an additional step at the first major press conference of his campaign against Nixon. He announced that he was appointing a two-man committee consisting of Senator Joseph Clark of Pennsylvania and Representative Emanuel Celler of New York who would propose a comprehensive civil rights bill based on the Democratic Party Platform for its introduction into Congress early in 1961. Kennedy promised to seek passage of the bill.[11]

During most of the campaign battle with Nixon, however, Kennedy placed less and less emphasis on new legislation. Instead he made a statement in the second television debate that the responsibility of the president was to provide "a moral tone and moral leadership" in the field of civil rights, and this became the dominant theme in the rest of the campaign. He said he thought the decision in *Brown* v. *Board of Education* (347 U.S. 483, 1954) was correct. He repeatedly pledged that upon assuming office he would ban discrimination in federally aided housing by executive order. He also promised more vigorous enforcement of the Civil Rights Acts of 1957 and 1960 to protect voting rights and efforts to end discrimination in government employment and by government contractors.[12]

In commenting about the election contest, Alexander Bickel has written:

In the course of this campaign, Mr. Kennedy and Mr. Nixon established a firm national consensus. and finally fixed the broad and pervasive principle of the School Segregation Cases of 1954 as not only the judicial but also the political policy of the federal government. The campaign established a new mood of executive engagement in the civil rights struggle and signalled an executive commitment to the morality of equal protection of the laws as a rule of independent, creative action, rather than as merely an obligation to uphold the courts.[13]

The election proved to be a very close one, and although civil rights was not a major issue, the Negro vote made a difference for Kennedy in several of the key states. The outcome of the Martin Luther King Jr. episode was an important factor in the Negro vote for Kennedy. King was one of the genuine heroes of the Negro struggle for equality in the United States because of his leadership in the non-violent movement to end discrimination. On October 19, 1960, he was arrested along with fifty-two other blacks for refusing to leave a segregated restaurant in Rich's department store in Atlanta. A few days later the others were released, but King was placed in a Georgia state prison after having been sentenced to four months at hard labor. There was considerable fear for King's safety. Several southern governors warned Kennedy against any intrusion on the grounds that it would doom the Democratic cause in the South. Nevertheless, Kennedy took the advice of Harris Wofford and telephoned Mrs. King to express his concern. Upon learning of the call, Robert Kennedy, his brother's campaign manager, telephoned the judge who had set the sentence and secured King's release on bond. This incident overcame the qualms of some of the black Protestant leaders about voting for a Catholic. Pamphlets were widely distributed on the eve of the election describing the incident, and there can be little doubt that it was instrumental in bringing about Kennedy's narrow victories in several states such as Michigan and Illinois.[14]

John F. Kennedy won the election by a very thin margin of a little over 100,000 in popular votes (49.7 percent of the total) and 303 to 219 in electoral votes. Interestingly enough, Nixon carried twenty-six states, Kennedy twenty-three states. (Mississippi voters cast most of their ballots for an independent slate of electors.) In Congress the Democrats retained control of both houses with a

262 to 175 margin in the House and a 65 to 35 margin in the Senate. One hundred and one of the Democrats in the House were elected from the South. The Democrats suffered net losses of two seats in the Senate and twenty in the House.

Theodore Sorensen, special counsel to President Kennedy, referred to the Eighty-Seventh Congress as the most conservative one elected in six years. The balance of power was held by a conservative coalition consisting of Republicans and southern Democrats. No bill could pass the House of Representatives without the support of some combination of forty-to-sixty southern Democrats or Republicans out of a total of seventy or so who were not intransigent on all issues. The situation was somewhat better in the Senate, but liberal Democrats possessed less than fifty percent of the votes.[15]

Besides the narrow victory and the problem of mustering a majority in Congress on any controversial issue, the Kennedy administration faced three additional obstructions in Congress: the House Rules Committee, Rule 22 in the Senate, and the committee chairmen in both houses. In the House the Rules Committee was chaired by arch-conservative Howard W. Smith, representative from Virginia. This committee consisted of twelve members (eight Democrats and four Republicans), and it could practically dictate what legislation would be considered by the House and under what conditions. It tended to be controlled by conservatives from both parties, and liberal legislation faced virtually certain blockage.

Because the House handled several thousand bills each year, important pieces of legislation—especially those favored by a committee or by the president—needed priority status. It was the special business of the Rules Committee to grant such priority. It could grant or withhold a special rule, and a bill without such a rule could easily be lost. The rule, once granted, could either facilitate or make difficult any effort to amend a bill on the House floor. In addition, the committee, by issuing a rule, could set the length of debate once a bill reached the floor for consideration. Finally, the committee, through the threat of withholding a special rule, could cause an alteration in a bill.

Faced with this obstruction to his entire program, the new president and his advisors decided to deal with it at the beginning of the session in 1961. White House officials joined with Speaker Sam Rayburn in gaining approval by the House for the enlargement of the committee to fifteen members, ten Democrats and five Republicans. This change provided the liberals with an eight to seven margin on most issues and thereby prevented conservative Republicans and southern Democrats on the committee from automatically blocking House floor action on most liberal administrative proposals approved by other committees.[16] Nevertheless, civil rights bills would still probably encounter insurmountable difficulty in obtaining approval by the committee.

In the Senate the president was faced with the ever-present threat of a filibuster. Through the virtually unlimited debate a small group of determined senators could either prevent the majority from holding sway or could long delay a majority decision on legislation. Any civil rights bill, an anathema to southern senators, was, of course, especially vulnerable to the filibuster. As matters stood, it was very difficult to cope with the filibuster because of Senate Rule 22. Under this rule a two-thirds vote of the senators present and voting was necessary to curb debate. This kind of majority was almost impossible to obtain for several reasons: (1) those favoring delay in a particular instance would be opposed to cloture; (2) the tradition of freedom of debate on the Senate floor was deeply ingrained in the thoughts of many senators; and (3) some would probably vote against cloture in the hopes that they would be aided by others they had helped when filibustering against another bill.

The Democrats had pledged in their 1960 platform to alter or abolish Rule 22 in favor of simple majority rule in the Senate, and the Republicans had promised a change too. Senate liberals decided to move against the two-thirds rule in January 1961, but White House aid was not forthcoming and the effort failed. Seeing little chance of success and believing that the filibuster was not a great threat except to civil rights bills, the administration apparently decided not to back the change for fear of antagonizing southern and western senators. The filibuster, therefore, remained a threat to any civil rights bill.

In addition, there was the matter of the committee chairmen in both houses. Committee chairmen were extremely powerful since they could exercise a large degree of control over the output of their committees. They controlled the hearings, the agenda, both rewards and punishments, and the committee's staff. Since seniority was the criterion for a chairmanship, many chairmen in both houses came from the South and Southwest as a result of being from one-party states. They tended to oppose new civil rights bills. Some of the southerners, especially Senator James Eastland of Mississippi and, of course, Smith from Virginia, chaired powerful committees—the Senate Judiciary and House Rules, respectively —that might deal with civil rights legislation.

In addition to the problems in Congress and his narrow electoral victory, President Kennedy faced a number of other difficulties. Among them was the situation in which the president might issue administrative or executive orders but could not always be certain that the bureaucracy would follow them in the way intended. The federal system itself contained certain built-in restraints in that there were certain areas in which the federal government was precluded from exercising power—e.g., much of the police power obtained at the local level. Moreover, laws passed by Congress sometimes contained restrictions on the executive branch, since they might specify what the executive could or could not do in given instances. Finally, the congressional power of the purse strings exercised in appropriation bills could provide restraints on executive actions—e.g., through not voting enough funds for an agency to fulfill its mission.

Despite these obstacles the president did have some important levers he might pull. These came within the province of his executive power for the most part and the prestige of his office. He could issue executive and administrative orders, give speeches in order to influence public opinion, use his personal influence to persuade governmental officials to enforce certain policies, make contacts with important persons outside government, make proposals to Congress, make use of his authority as commander-in-chief to effect changes in the armed forces and the communities in which they served, call on the armed forces to enforce court orders, employ his own power of the purse, encourage or threaten litigation in the courts, make effective use of the appointive power, and discourage federal officials from attending segregated gatherings so that they would serve as examples for the rest of society.

The black leaders had great expectations and hoped that the new administration would move forcefully to remove the inequities in American society. Martin Luther King and Roy Wilkins, among others, presented their proposals to President Kennedy, and some leaders wrote about their requests for action in journals and pamphlets. As indicative of what the Negro leaders were thinking, King explained in an article for the *Nation* that the time was past for tolerating vicious opposition on a subject which affected the lives of twenty-million Americans. He insisted that the slow pace of progress was due as much to the limits the federal government had imposed on itself as it was to the actions of the segregationists. He complained that the federal government was financing racial segregation, while pointing out that taxes were collected from all citizens regardless of race. He called for a number of changes and asked for the president to mobilize the nation's resources to eliminate discrimination as Roosevelt had done to cope with the depression.[17]

The Southern Regional Council, a leading civil rights organization based in Atlanta, issued a report early in 1961 which was apparently studied by President Kennedy. The authors of the report also urged immediate and far-reaching steps to eliminate discrimination against the Negroes. They insisted that the American president "holds power under the Constitution and existing statutes which, diligently exercised, could carry the country far toward racial relations that are sane and honorable. These powers should be examined and responsibly used."[18]

The report also pointed out that although the courts had secured the enforcement of many of the Negroes' rights, the judicial process was not an adequate substitute for political leadership. The nation needed to feel "the impulse of Presidential concern and activity."[19] The authors recommended a number of specific changes such as a housing order and the ending of other areas of federal assistance to segregationist practices. At the end of the report they declared that the chief executive "is the center of American energy. What the President says and does will mark the direction and the speed with which the country moves to perfect its racial relations."[20]

Both President Kennedy and his brother Robert, who was attorney general, had certain attitudes of their own toward civil rights for Negroes. According to Theodore Sorensen the president's primary interest had always been in foreign policy before he assumed the presidency. He noted that until Kennedy became president, he thought of the blacks largely in terms of votes.[21] Harry Golden wrote that "I do not think that either the late President or the Attorney General was fully aware of the enormity of those wrongs when they took their oaths of office."[22] Another writer, Margaret Laing, declared that the president seemed to have a terrible ambivalence about civil rights, and that Robert Kennedy was emotionally uncommitted when he took his cabinet post. When asked in an interview what area he would concentrate on in the Justice Department, Robert Kennedy stated that it would be organized crime. He did point out, however, that he thought civil rights would be the most difficult field.[23] Perhaps Golden summarized the attorney general's position best when he wrote:

There is no doubt that Robert Kennedy envisioned his role in his brother's administration mainly as the Attorney General who would prosecute James R. Hoffa, boss of the Teamsters' Union. Swearing the oath of office Robert F. Kennedy had no idea that the pursuit of James Hoffa would become insignificant compared to his work preparing fifty-eight civil rights cases in addition to the inspection of voting records in over one hundred counties in his first thirty months as the Attorney General.[24]

Given their attitudes and the other factors such as black expectations and campaign promises, the president was in a difficult situation. Special Assistant Arthur M. Schlesinger, Jr., noted that:

While he did not doubt the depth of the injustice or the need for remedy, he had read the arithmetic of the new Congress and concluded that there was no possible chance of passing a civil rights bill. Moreover, he had a wider range of presidential responsibilities and a fight for civil rights would alienate southern support he needed for other purposes (including bills, like those for education and the increased minimum wage, of direct benefit to the Negro). And he feared that the inevitable defeat of a civil rights bill after debate and filibuster would heighten Negro resentment, drive the civil rights revolution to more drastic resorts and place a perhaps intolerable strain on the already fragile social fabric. He therefore settled on the strategy of executive action.[25]

This decision inevitably caused a number of black leaders to be quite critical of the president's procrastination about fulfilling his campaign pledges. However, the president hoped to offset any discontent with a number of less important but still significant steps.

The broad outline of the civil rights strategy of the new administration as established early in 1961 was as follows:

1. No new legislation would be sought; instead the expanded use of executive power would be stressed.

2. Executive action would be undertaken only in those fields in which federal authority was most complete and undisputed. The administration would work cautiously in the area of federal-state relations, especially with respect to financial assistance. Sanctions would be imposed only as a last resort after long efforts at conciliation and persuasion failed.

3. The president's personal influence and prestige would be utilized sparingly. Robert Kennedy, as the president's brother and attorney general, would be the chief strategist and the acknowledged leader of the civil rights activities within the federal government.

4. Top priority would be given to the Negroes' right to vote. It was felt that other rights flowed from the exercise of the franchise. The Civil Rights Division of the Department of Justice would employ both negotiation and litigation to attain this end.[26]

This strategy was, of course, subject to change. In fact, black militancy, southern white resistance, and a number of critical episodes would bring alterations as time passed.

# 3. The JFK Administration and Its Assault upon Discrimination

In this chapter the focus centers on the president's exercise of power in a number of different areas of discrimination. Before delving into the actual use of executive tools, it is appropriate that we first examine the organization that was created by the new president and his advisors to deal with the Negro problem.

The president's brother, Robert Kennedy, who was attorney general in the new administration, gave overall direction to the administration's civil rights policies. Major questions of policy and execution to cope with large-scale problems were dealt with by him and his staff. Robert Kennedy was ably assisted by Burke Marshall, assistant attorney general, who was the head of the Civil Rights Division in the Department of Justice. Mention should also be made of Byron White, who served as deputy attorney general until 1962 when he was appointed to the Supreme Court, and of Nicholas Katzenbach, who succeeded White.

Organizationally speaking, the hub of the wheel was the president's Subcabinet Group on Civil Rights. Each federal agency—the Civil Rights Commission, the cabinet departments, the General Services Administration, and a host of others—sent a high-ranking official (at the assistant secretary level) to the subcabinet group. It met once a month in the White House under the chairmanship of Harris Wofford, Jr., President Kennedy's special assistant for civil rights. Wofford was replaced by Lee White, special assistant counsel to the president, in 1962.[1]

In addition to the Subcabinet Group on Civil Rights, there was an ad hoc committee that met frequently and informally. Its members discussed ongoing programs and proposed solutions for emergencies.[2] This committee assisted Wofford with tactical and administrative problems on which he advised the president and the sub-cabinet group and provided a forum for orderly discussion and communication of policy affecting all or a considerable number of agencies. In time, however, the ad hoc group fell into disuse, and its role was assumed to some extent by the staff members of the Civil Rights Commission. The Civil Rights Commission itself had been established as a result of the Civil Rights Act of 1957. As outlined by Congress, the commission's responsibilities were to investigate complaints of citizens deprived of their right to vote by reason of color, race, national origin, or religion; to appraise federal policies in the general field of legal enforcement of the Fourteenth Amendment; and to collect information on legal developments constituting a denial of equal protection of the laws.

Gradually the subcabinet group's sessions grew less and less frequent as more and more of the agencies developed their own civil rights concerns. Moreover, the subcabinet group proved too large for efficient discussion, and many of the issues were too varied to permit a common focus on them.[3]

Let us now proceed to examine some of the areas where the Kennedy Administration attempted to assault discriminatory practices.

## Major Federal Appointments of Blacks

In order to communicate to the general public as well as to the Negroes that the administration was ready to choose persons for important governmental posts on the basis of merit without regard to other considerations, President Kennedy appointed a number of Negroes to such posts. Robert C. Weaver was named to head the Housing and Home Finance Agency; George Weaver was made assistant secretary of labor; Carl T. Rowan was named assistant secretary of state for public affairs; Andrew Hatcher was appointed associate press secretary; Lisle Carter was appointed as deputy assistant secretary in the Department of Health, Education, and Welfare; and Frank Reeves was named to the White House staff.

For the first time blacks were named as ambassadors to European as well as African countries. Clifton Wharton was appointed as ambassador to Norway, and he was the first Negro to serve as ambassador to a predominantly white country and the first of his race to rise through the career service to become an ambassador.

The president also appointed blacks as federal judges. The most prestigious appointment was that of Thurgood Marshall, who was named as a judge on the Second Circuit Court of Appeals. Moreover, Kennedy appointed the first two Negroes to be federal district judges in the United States. Mrs. Marjorie Lawson was the first Negro woman to be appointed to the federal bench—as a federal judge in Washington, D.C.

Other important appointments were made by the president. Spottswood Robinson III was made a member of the Civil Rights Commission. John Duncan was appointed as a commissioner for the District of Columbia. Finally, A. Leon Higginbotham was named to the Federal Trade Commission, the first Negro to serve on a federal regulatory agency.

For the most part the Negro appointees encountered little difficulty in being confirmed by the Senate, since the president nominated hardly any Negroes who were prominent in the civil rights movement from the South. An exception was Robert C. Weaver, whose nomination was vehemently opposed by a number of southern senators and by the National Municipal Association. Part of the reason for so much opposition was that it was clear from the outset that he was likely to be chosen as the secretary of the new Department of Urban Affairs and Housing. Though Weaver was confirmed, strong southern opposition presaged trouble for any attempt to establish such a department.

Frank Reeves, a member of the White House staff, was nominated as a commissioner for Washington, D.C., but his name was withdrawn when it was discovered that he was delinquent in paying his income taxes. He was also released from the White House staff. The only other Negro to encounter considerable opposition was Spottswood Robinson III, who was appointed to the Civil Rights Commission. He was a native Virginian and had served as counsel for the NAACP, but over the protest of a number of southern senators he was easily confirmed for the post.

Concerning the appointments, a report of the Southern Regional Council read:

It is probably noteworthy and commendable that the Kennedy Administration has been willing to appoint to high office Negroes who have been leaders of the civil rights movement. It is noteworthy also, however, that very few of the appointments have come from the South. The administration has avoided challenges to southern power by appointing very few Negro southerners prominent in the civil rights movement to high office, the principal exception being Mr. Spottswood Robinson of the Commission on Civil Rights.[4]

The Negro vote had been of great importance in the president's election. It was in harmony with American political tradition and practice that the role of the Negroes in the election would have established the Negro's right to some of the spoils of victory. Kennedy paid off his political debt, and in so doing he brought into office blacks of recognized distinction and ability.

## Social and Moral Support

The president, in order to set the tone for the country and the governmental policies of his administration, ordered his leading advisors and cabinet officers to avoid segregated meetings and facilities. When Robert Kennedy, together with a number of important friends and officials, resigned from the prestigious Metropolitan Club in Washington since it discriminated against blacks, the president told a news conference that he approved of what they had done.[5]

Theodore Sorensen wrote a story about how Arthur Krock of the *New York Times,* when informed of the president's attitude, remarked that the rules of the Metropolitan Club were none of the president's business. When Krock later found that the administration was deliberately excluding Moise Tshombe, Congolese rebel leader from appearing in the United States, he was infuriated. The president, speaking at a Gridiron Club dinner, replied by telling the members that he would invite Tshombe to the United States if Krock would invite him to the Metropolitan Club.[6]

To cite another example, in 1961 the Civil War Centennial Commission planned segregated housing for its membership during a session at Charleston, South Carolina. Upon learning of this arrangement, the president became very annoyed and persuaded its chairman, U. S. Grant III, to shift the meetings to the unsegregated naval station.[7]

The steps taken by the administration to give social and moral support to the cause of nondiscrimination were of symbolic importance to the Negro. The Kennedy administration, through its own actions, was practicing what it preached and serving as an example for the rest of society to follow.

## Transportation

In the spring of 1961 James Farmer and CORE sent out groups of "freedom riders" from Washington, D. C., to the South on two buses to challenge segregation in interstate bus terminals—in restaurants, restrooms, and waiting rooms. There was no trouble until they entered Alabama. One of the buses was burned outside Anniston, and some riders were beaten. They continued to Birmingham and were beaten again. Birmingham police had been warned in advance by federal officials that the riders were coming, and it had been requested that police protection be furnished, but this plea was to no avail. The police arrived on the scene too late. The Justice Department then became involved.

When a new group of "freedom riders" set out for Montgomery, Attorney General Kennedy sought and received assurances from Alabama Governor John Patterson that they would have state protection. Nevertheless, mob violence took place again in Montgomery, and the attorney general then dispatched some six hundred deputy marshals to the scene. At this point the violence began to subside.

In the meantime federal officials arrested nine persons allegedly responsible for the violence at Anniston, and they were held for trial. When asked about these events at a press conference, the president declared that the "Attorney General has made it clear that we believe everyone who travels, for whatever reason they travel, should enjoy the full constitutional protection given to them by the law and the Constitution."[8]

As a result of these episodes the president asked the attorney general to petition the Interstate Commerce Commission for remedial action. A precedent for this strategy had been established in 1955 when the ICC ordered thirteen railroad companies and one bus company to cease all segregation practices. That part of the order dealing with the bus company concerned only bus-seating and not service in the terminals. In the case of the railroads the order did relate to terminals except in one instance, a terminal lessee.[9] However, state and municipal officials in the South prevented the railroads from carrying out the order.

An additional precedent for the Kennedy Administration's strategy occurred when the Supreme Court in *Boynton* v. *Virginia* (364 U.S. 454, 1960) placed interstate bus terminals within the desegregation policy stemming from the Interstate Commerce Act. Moreover, by implication the court reversed the reasoning of the ICC in its earlier exemption of a terminal restaurant lessee from the desegregation order.[10]

Armed with ample precedents, therefore, Robert Kennedy initiated the action on May 29, 1961. He requested the ICC to issue regulations requiring desegregation of all facilities in terminals used in interstate bus travel. In this document the Justice Department also furnished a text of suggested regulations to fulfill the terms of the petition.

In addition, both Robert McNamara, the secretary of defense, and Dean Rusk, the secretary of state, sent letters supporting the petition. Secretary Rusk, as might be expected, stressed the damage caused by segregated transportation to America's image abroad. He wrote: "I hope that the action now being sought will significantly advance the purpose of achieving non-discriminatory and equal treatment for all persons traveling in the United States."[11]

The ICC held hearings on August 15, 1961, and at that time the Justice Department presented the result of an FBI survey which showed, among other things, that there were widespread segregation signs in southern terminals. The commission was impressed, and the proposed regulations included in the petition were in essence adopted by the ICC. This action constituted one of those very rare examples of the "executive branch's taking the initiative in requesting specific action from an independent regulatory commission possessed of rule-making powers, on a specific policy matter —complete with a blueprint for action."[12]

The ICC order was issued on September 22, 1961, but did not go into effect until November 1, 1961. Until January 1, 1963, signs on buses were to be displayed stating: "Seating aboard this vehicle is without regard to race, color, creed, or national origin, by order of the Interstate Commerce Commission."[13] After January 1, 1963, the nondiscrimination statement was to be printed on tickets. In the meantime, signs in terminals calling for nondiscrimination were to be prominently displayed immediately.[14]

The crucial section of the ICC order was worded as follows:

No motor common carrier of passengers . . . shall in the operation of vehicles in interstate or foreign commerce provide, maintain arrangements for, utilize, make available, adhere to any understanding for the availability of, any terminal facilities which are so operated, arranged, or maintained as to involve any separation of any portion thereof on the basis of race, color, creed, or national origin.[15]

Following the issuance of this order, the Department of Justice tried negotiations to carry out its terms on the buses and if that did not work litigation was used.

Concurrently with these actions the Department of Justice undertook negotiations with eighteen leading southern railroads for the purpose of desegregating all rail facilities. In mid-October 1961 a verbal arrangement was announced. By January 1962 written agreements were obtained from all rail lines serving the South.[16] A large number of local rail terminals carried out the agreement. However, wherever state interference was attempted, the Department of Justice quickly resorted to the federal courts under the authority of the Interstate Commerce Act.

The Department of Justice also took the initiative in the area of air transportation. There was no real problem aboard planes but there was with airport facilities. The leading case was *United States* v. *City of Montgomery* (201 F. Supp. 590, 1962) which was filed in June 1961. Two bases were asserted by the department for this action and they were accepted by the federal district judge in deciding for the government: (1) the principle derived from *In re Debs* (158 U.S. 564, 1895) of an executive power to safeguard interstate commerce without any need for a statute; and (2) that upon request by the aviation agencies the Justice Department might enforce substantive standards specified by a regulation or a statute, including a nondiscrimination clause.[17]

Armed with victory in the City of Montgomery case, Robert Kennedy instituted an FBI survey of 165 commercially operated airports in the United States, and as a result it was found that segregation was widely practiced in seven states. Both the Civil Aeronautics Board and the Federal Aviation Agency exerted pressure, and the Justice Department handled the negotiations with appropriate airport officials. Letters were sent out out in the spring of 1962 by Assistant Attorney General Burke Marshall and voluntary desegregation was achieved with three exceptions—New Orleans, Birmingham, and Shreveport. A private suit was already pending in New Orleans and by mid-summer of 1962 desegregation was accomplished there. In the other two instances, suits were filed by the Department of Justice and successfully concluded on the basis of the earlier Montgomery decision.[18]

While there were pockets of segregation remaining in interstate transportation facilities, the battle was largely won. By 1963 Attorney General Kennedy could report that virtually every airport as well as bus and railroad station in the South had been desegregated.[19]

## Public Housing

President Kennedy had promised to ban segregation in federally owned or assisted public housing during the 1960 campaign with a stroke of the pen. Undoubtedly, for political reasons, he did not consider the time propitious for the order for many months. The president wanted to protect other programs, and, of course, to achieve the elevation of Robert Weaver to cabinet status as secretary of the new Department of Urban Affairs and Housing from his position as head of the Housing and Home Finance Agency. Weaver was a Negro and an advocate of open occupancy. The president's proposal was defeated in 1961 and again in early 1962.[20]

Nothing of note happened in 1961 to improve the situation in housing. On April 7, 1962, the Urban Renewal Administration announced that builders would thereafter be required to comply with provisions of local and state laws which prohibited discrimination in the sale or rental of homes because of color, race, religion, or national origin.[21]

After much clamoring from civil rights groups, the president at last announced the signing of the housing order at a news conference on November 20, 1962. To assist federal agencies and departments in enforcing it, he declared that he had established the President's Committee on Equal Opportunity in Housing. The president stated that it was neither proper nor equitable that American citizens should be denied the benefits of federally owned housing (or housing financed through federal assistance) for reason of race, color, creed, or national origin.[22]

The executive order was called "Equal Opportunity in Housing." Under its terms the president directed federal agencies to take every proper and legal action to prevent discrimination in (1) the sale or leasing of housing which was owned or operated by the federal government; (2) housing which was constructed or sold through loans which were made, insured, or guaranteed by the federal government; and (3) housing which was made available through slum clearance or urban renewal programs.[23]

The housing order was concerned most directly with future housing. Probably one-fourth of all future housing in the United States would be affected. Where housing constructed with federal aid was already built, governmental agencies were asked to "use their good offices" to prevent discrimination, but there was no way to force owners to comply as no governmental sanctions were available.[24]

The president's housing order did not cover conventionally financed housing, even that part in which funds for the loans were insured by the FDIC, as with the saving and loan associations. As Sorensen pointed out, "To prevent its being tied up in a long legal battle and other complex reasons (including no control over a key banking agency), the order provided only for voluntary efforts with respect to housing already built and housing financed by conventional bank mortgages. . . . The predicted disruptions and decline in home-building and Federal financing never materialized."[25]

The various housing agencies of the federal government carried out the executive order with some softening. Federal agencies, for instance, did not cover the sale or rental of one-family or two-family houses occupied by the owner except in instances where a black was denied a loan on racial grounds after an owner had approved sale or rental to him. In addition, in an attempt at moral suasion, the Federal Home Loan Bank Board adopted a resolution opposing racial discrimination in mortgage lending by the 1,873 saving and loan associations that it supervised.[26]

Harold Fleming, executive vice president of the Potomac Institute in Washington, D.C., and former executive director of the Southern Regional Council, made the following assessment in 1965:

> The order did contain a "good offices" provision, Section 102, under which the housing agencies were directed to take appropriate action permitted by law, including the institution of appropriate litigation, if required, to promote the abandonment of discriminatory legislation with respect to residential property and related facilities heretofore provided with Federal financial assistance. . . . With few exceptions in the realm of persuasion, mostly ineffective, this approach to existing housing has not been used. Not a single law suit has been filed to implement it. The net effect of the order was to bring under the nondiscrimination requirement less than 20% of the new housing starts annually. When the turnover of existing units is considered, this is only a small fraction of the housing market in a given year.[27]

## Armed Forces

Discrimination in the armed forces, as in every level of American society, was a fact of life when John F. Kennedy took office in 1961. Considerable strides had been made as the result of actions taken by presidents Truman and Eisenhower. Although the services were undoubtedly integrated to a greater extent than civilian life, there were still many shortcomings. The reserve units were also not integrated, and no real progress had been made in the National Guard. Outside the base the Negro serviceman and his family found segregation rampant in many parts of the country.

An indication of the new president's interest was manifested by his anger over the fact that in his inaugural parade no Negro coast guardsman took part. Kennedy found that the Coast Guard was virtually all white, and he immediately took steps to remedy that situation after he was sworn in as president of the United States.

In September 1961 the Defense Department urged army commanders to make continuing efforts through command-community relations committees to obtain non-segregated housing off base. However, in practice, military personnel and their families were told by their commanders to observe local customs and laws outside of military installations.[28]

As of 1961 there were still six Negro reserve units in the Army. On April 3, 1962, Roswell Gilpatrick, the deputy secretary of defense for manpower, ordered them integrated. In June 1963 the Pentagon announced that the integration of the reserves had been achieved, but token integration remained the norm in the National Guard.[29]

In the meantime the President's Commission on Civil Rights urged that a study be made of discrimination in the armed services. On June 22, 1962, President Kennedy appointed the Committee on Equal Opportunity in the Armed Forces under the chairmanship of Gerhard A. Gesell. In his letter to Gesell, the president stressed that the Department of Defense had made great progress toward eliminating discrimination. He thought, however, that the time had come for a review of the situation both within the services and in communities where military installations were located in order to determine what additional steps were necessary to assure equality of treatment in the armed services. The president asked that the committee consider, along with the general problem, two specific questions:

1. What measures should be taken to improve the effectiveness of current policies and procedures in the Armed Forces with regard to equality of treatment and opportunity for persons in the Armed Forces?

2. What measures should be employed to improve the equality of opportunity for members of the Armed Forces and their dependents in the civilian community, particularly with respect to housing, education, transportation, recreational facilities, community events, programs and activities?[30]

The first report of this committee was issued on June 13, 1963. The Gesell committee worked closely with the Civil Rights Commission in making its investigation. Among other things, the committee found that although eleven percent of the American population was Negro, only 8.2 percent of all military personnel were black. The situation was worse in the U. S. Navy, where only one percent of the Navy's enlisted men were Negroes. In all of the services the percentage of officers was low. As of 1962 3.2 percent of the officers in the Army were Negroes; 1.2 percent in the Air Force; .2 percent in the Navy; and .2 percent in the Marines.[31] Very little progress had been made since 1948 when President Truman issued his executive order to the effect that Negroes should be able to advance into the higher ranks at either the enlisted or officer levels.

By and large, on the military bases there was a clear pattern of integration. At the same time, however,

Negro military personnel and their families are suffering humiliation and degradation in communities near the bases at which they are compelled to serve, and a vigorous new action is required to relieve the situation. In addition remaining problems of equality of treatment and opportunity, both service-wide and at particular bases, call for correction. National policy requires prompt action to eliminate all these conditions. Equal opportunity for the Negro will exist only when it is possible for him to enter upon a career of military service with assurance that his acceptance and his progress will be in no way impeded by reason of his color. Clearly distinctions based on race prevent full utilization of Negro military personnel and are inconsistent with the objectives of our democratic society.[32]

The Gesell report made major recommendations dealing with the following areas: (1) improvement of the participation of the Negro in the armed services; (2) elimination of remaining on-base discrimination; (3) the elimination of serious off-base discrimination by civilian communities affecting the morale of Negro military personnel and dependents; (4) the improvement of educational opportunities for Negro military personnel and their dependents; and (5) the improvement of off-base housing conditions. The recommendations concerned with off-base discrimination emphasized that efforts at negotiation be attempted by the base commanders with community leaders. There was the possibility of selective sanctions in establishing off-limits areas in a community; but, as the report noted: "Should all other efforts fail, the services must consider a curtailment or termination of activities at certain military installations near communities where discrimination is particularly prevalent. . . . The objective here shall be preservation of morale, not the punishment of local communities which have a tradition of segregation."[33]

In order to effectuate nondiscriminatory policies the Gesell committee declared that:

It will be necessary to establish offices in each service to monitor developments and to provide assistance. . . . Overall policies must be guided by an official within the Department of Defense whose full-time responsibility is the program for assuring equality of opportunity and treatment for servicemen. This official should have a full-time, biracial staff skilled in dealing with deprivations of equality, and should, in addition, have access to consultants who have broad experience in dealing with racial discrimination. Procedures must be devised to bring the base commander into close working relationship with other Federal bodies concerned with problems in this area, and with local groups working to eliminate forms of discrimination. All of the resources of the Federal Government should be available to him and brought to bear on the intelligent solution of specific problems.[34]

After the President received the report he sent it to Robert McNamara, the secretary of defense, with an accompanying letter dated June 21, 1963. In his letter President Kennedy wrote that: "The recommendations regarding both off-base and on-base conditions merit your prompt attention and certainly are in the spirit that I believe should characterize our approach to the matter. I would hope your review and report on the recommendations could be completed within 30 days."[35]

On July 26, 1963, McNamara sent out a directive to all those under his department. In the document the secretary noted that it was the responsibility of each military commander to oppose discriminatory practices affecting his men and their dependents in order to foster equal opportunity for them not only in areas under his immediate command but also in nearby communities. The primary responsibility for overseeing the program was assigned to the assistant secretary of defense (manpower) who would be assisted by an office of deputy assistant secretary of defense (civil rights). The military departments were told to issue instructions, manuals, and regulations as approved by the assistant secretary of defense. Each military commander was given responsibility for carrying out the intent of the directive. However, the commander could not employ "off-limits" sanctions without the approval of the secretary of his department. Finally, the military departments were expected to submit an outline of their program for implementation of the directive no later than August 15, 1963.[36]

Without waiting until August 15, the Defense Department issued a new series of directives: (1) base commanders in fifteen southern and border states were asked to aid families of their men to enter their children into unsegregated schools; (2) contracts were cancelled with those morticians who refused to guarantee services on a nonsegregated basis; and (3) the secretary banned participation by athletic teams and military bands and the use of equipment and military units in any off-base events if the audiences were segregated.[37]

Altogether some significant steps were taken by the Kennedy Administration to deal with discrimination in the armed services.

The integration of the reserves had been accomplished and some significant actions were underway to deal with both on-base and off-base discrimination as a result of the recommendations made by the Gesell committee. No real progress had been made, however, in the National Guard.

## Voting

Voting was still a great problem for the black, particularly in the South. Under the Civil Rights Acts of 1957 and 1960 steps could be taken by the Justice Department to bring about some improvement. According to Alexander Bickel, during the Eisenhower Administration the Justice Department filed six suits; one was settled, two others were tried, and the other three had not yet gone to trial when the new administration came in.[38] The Kennedy administration gave the right of the Negroes' use of the franchise rather high priority on the grounds that the vote was the key to other rights.

A study was made by the Justice Department in 1961, and it was found that in at least 193 counties in the South less than fifteen percent of the eligible Negroes could register to vote. This was the case in seventy-four out of eighty-two counties in Mississippi. Since the Kennedy strategy called for no new legislation, at least in the beginning, heavy reliance would be placed on the enforcement of existing laws by the Justice Department.

Early in 1961 the Justice Department stopped the eviction of Negro farmers in Haywood and Fayette Counties, Tennessee, who were being punished for their voting activity in 1960. In addition, federal surplus foods were sent to aid the victims during the waiting period until litigation had been completed.[39]

While the Justice Department lawyers were filing an increasing number of voting suits, they were handicapped by weaknesses in the Civil Rights Act of 1957 and 1960. On the average it took twenty-eight months of preparation on each case before it was completed. At that rate it would take many years before a serious dent could be made in the disenfranchisement of the Negro.[40]

For that reason the administration decided to support legislation designed to eliminate the literacy test in federal elections. In his state of the union address in January 1962 the president mentioned the need for such legislation. On January 25, 1962, the Mansfield-Dirksen bill was introduced into the Senate. The bill followed the general outlines of a recommendation made by the Civil Rights Commission that a sixth grade standard would be considered an adequate test of literacy for voting. However, while the commission recommendation included state elections, the Mansfield-Dirksen bill did not. Civil Rights Commissioner Griswold and Attorney General Kennedy were among those who testified for the bill at the hearings before the Constitutional Rights Subcommittee of the Senate Judiciary Committee. Ultimately the bill was defeated since the Senate twice refused to shut off a filibuster by southerners against the motion to reconsider.[41]

President Kennedy had also proposed that the right to vote not be denied by such devices as the poll tax in his state of the union message. In March 1962 the Senate gave its approval to a constitutional amendment by the requisite majority, and the House followed in August.[42] The amendment barred the payment of the poll tax for voting in federal elections and primaries. This was not a very far-reaching step for several reasons: (1) the poll tax existed only in Alabama, Mississippi, Texas, Virginia, and Arkansas; (2) the poll tax was not the major obstacle to Negro voting even in those states where it existed; and (3) the amendment did not include state elections and primaries. In any case the amendment was later adopted by the requisite number of states, and it became a part of the Constitution. Moreover, in 1966, the Supreme Court declared state poll taxes violative of the Fourteenth Amendment in *Harper* v. *Va. State Bd. of Elections* (383 U.S. 663, 1966).

In the meantime, the Department of Justice continued the slow and tedious litigation process in order to enfranchise the Negro. In June 1962 Attorney General Kennedy announced that investigations and court action under the Civil Rights Acts of 1957 and 1960 were underway in almost one hundred counties. Twenty-two voting suits had been filed since the administration had taken office. For the first time a number of suits had been filed against

Mississippi counties. Even Sunflower County, the home of Senator James Eastland, was not exempt.[43]

Moreover, on July 24, 1962, twenty-six Negroes from East Carroll Parish in Northeast Louisiana were registered to vote by a federal judge in the first proceeding of its kind under the Civil Rights Act of 1960. On August 28, 1962, the Department of Justice filed a complaint in the federal district court in Jackson, Mississippi. It asked the court to declare unconstitutional two sections of the Mississippi State Constitution which required interpretation tests and "good moral character," and it made a similar request concerning seven state laws which set up other devices to discriminate against prospective Negro voters.[44]

On another front the Justice Department encouraged the civil rights organizations to engage in voter registration drives. They were reluctant at first, out of suspicion that the department was trying to divert their attention from more important efforts. They finally agreed, however. In the early summer of 1962 the Southern Regional Council announced the formation of the Voter Education Project. Other organizations deciding to participate were the NAACP the National Urban League, SNCC, CORE, and the Southern Christian Leadership Conference. The Justice Department worked closely with these groups and attempted to protect their workers through the courts.

With substantial support from private philanthropic foundations, a tremendous effort was made to train Negroes in the complexities of registration in hostile communities and to encourage them to use their vote. The drive was met with white harassment, police brutality, and considerable violence, including the burning of three Negro churches. Nevertheless, as a result of these and other efforts, some 90,000 Negroes were registered to vote by the early fall of 1962. This raised the total to 1,500,000 registered Negro voters in the South out of a potential registration of over 5,000,000.[45]

Most of the gains occurred in the cities where there were relatively few obstacles. In the small towns and rural districts the Negroes encountered great difficulties in attempting to register, as did workers for the Voter Education Project in efforts to fulfill their mission. The registration effort continued into 1963, though increasingly stiff resistance was offered, particularly in Mississippi. Only active intervention by federal officials made it possible for them to continue. By the end of 1963, through the efforts of the Voter Education Project in part, some 688,800 more persons were added to the registration rolls in two and one-half years in the South and many of them were Negroes.[46]

The Department of Justice continued to file suits in 1963. By the end of that year the department had filed a total of fifty-eight voting suits (including those under Eisenhower); thirty-three of them had been tried, nineteen won by the government, and the rest were on appeal. Suits had been filed in every major metropolitan area in the South. Negroes were registered in about a dozen southern counties where none had been previously registered. In another ten counties a fairly large number were registered where only a few were on the rolls earlier.[47]

## Education

Unlike Dwight Eisenhower, President Kennedy declared at the outset his approval of the school desegregation cases. He was joined in his endorsement by the attorney general. An innovation occurred when the Kennedy administration abandoned the position of the Eisenhower administration that it would become involved in litigation only at a judge's invitation to enforce a court order. In 1960 the Justice Department had rejected a federal judge's request for help in Louisiana to assist in planning the desegregation of schools in that state. In 1961 all federal judges were put on notice that the government intended to carry out the Constitution and court orders regardless "of the political consequences."[48] Two months after assuming office, Attorney General Kennedy brought the federal government into two Louisiana school suits as an *amicus curiae* to contest some new state laws obstructing desegregation. This step was unprecedented since it was taken without an invitation and without any immediate threat of violence to frustrate the enforcement of a court order.[49]

Not all federal judges were amenable to federal governmental participation in school desegregation suits. For instance, Robert Kennedy had sought to enter the litigation in Prince Edward County, Virginia, where all public schools had been closed since 1959 to evade a court order calling for desegregation. In this case the federal judge refused to admit the Justice Department to the suit. However, the department in cooperation with private sources was able to establish a temporary "free" school in 1963 which brought about a return of education for young blacks.[50]

Still another precedent was established in New Rochelle, New York, in May 1961. The Justice Department was invited by the federal district court to serve as a friend of the court. Representatives of the federal government did intervene, and they submitted a brief disapproving of a desegregation plan already drawn by the local school board and suggesting guidelines for a new plan. For the first time the Justice Department had intervened not to protect United States sovereignty or to advise the court of constitutional matters. The district court adopted a plan closely corresponding to the guidelines suggested by the Justice Department and the Court of Appeals affirmed the decision of the district court.[51]

During the spring of 1961 important but unpublicized work was carried on by Burke Marshall and John Siegenthaler, Robert Kennedy's special assistant. They toured the South and held quiet and informed consultation with local officials in twenty-three school districts. At times Robert Kennedy would help with a telephone call to an official. As a result, in the fall of 1961, schools in New Orleans, Atlanta, Memphis, and Dallas were partially desegregated. The president publicly praised the appropriate officials in these cities.[52]

On still another front, early in 1962, Abraham Ribicoff, the secretary of health, education, and welfare, announced that effective September 1963 the federal government would regard segregated schools as unsuitable for children whose parents lived and worked on federal installations. If school districts persisted in their policies of segregation, Ribicoff declared that his department would set up schools on the installations and terminate "impacted area" aid to the offending school districts.[53]

On September 17, 1962, to supplement to Secretary Ribicoff's action, the Justice Department filed a law suit in the federal district court in Richmond, Virginia, to end racial discrimination in the Prince George County public schools. Fort Lee, a major army base, was located in the county, and impacted aid was received for the public schools. This marked the first time that the federal government had initiated a school desegregation suit. It was an important case for private groups, because they foresaw that the financial burden of instituting and prosecuting civil rights cases might be shifted to the federal government in those parts of the South which benefited from impacted area aid.[54]

In the meantime, in February 1962, the Department of Health, Education, and Welfare made a significant decision affecting higher education. The United States commissioner of education announced that language and counseling institutes held under the auspices of the National Defense Education Act would not be sponsored at colleges and universities not accepting Negroes as enrollees in 1962. After the institutes were held in the summer of 1962, it was found that eleven colleges in the South had Negroes attending institutes for the first time, and for four of them it was the first breach of the segregational barrier in the schools. Following this example, the National Science Foundation announced that it would pursue the same policy with its institutes in 1963.[55]

At a different level the United States Office of Education took additional steps in 1962. As a part of its annual review of state vocational education programs which were supported by federal funds, this office inquired for the first time into the availability of that type of training for different races in the school districts receiving federal funds.[56] In addition the same agency made plans to establish a clearing house to help local school officials plan for desegregation. This project was expected to be under way in time for the new school year.[57]

The most dramatic episode in the field of education was the break of the color barrier in Mississippi in the Meredith case in the fall of 1962. A federal court order was issued for James Meredith's admission into the University of Mississippi, but it required strong action by the federal government to ensure his enrollment as a result of defiance on the part of Governor Ross Barnett and a large number of students at the university.[58]

Upon learning of the court order, Governor Barnett warned that no school would be integrated while he was governor. Moreover, he resorted to the unlawful doctrine of interposition in his rhetorical effort to block what he referred to as interference on the part of the federal government in the internal affairs of Mississippi.[59]

Nevertheless, on September 30, 1962, Meredith was brought to Ole Miss accompanied by federal marshals. During the worst part of the crisis the president, together with the attorney general, maintained a constant vigilance as events unfolded. They had many telephone conversations with their representatives on the scene and with Governor Barnett. Ironically, just as the president addressed the nation that same night, to plead with Mississippi students not to interfere, violence erupted.

In order to carry out the court order, it was necessary for the Justice Department to dispatch 541 United States marshals, and the president alerted several thousand federal troops and federalized the Mississippi National Guard. Federal troops were retained in Oxford for the rest of the year to maintain order and to protect Meredith as he completed requirements for a degree.[60]

The next year, on June 11, 1963, two Negroes, Vivian Malone and James Hood, were registered as students at the University of Alabama. This was the first desegregation of a public institution in that state. Governor George Wallace had stated that he would defy the federal court, and the administration feared that another episode of the magnitude of the Meredith case might take place. Governor Wallace refused to permit the registration on the morning of June 11, and then the president signed an executive order federalizing the Alabama National Guard. Then, confronted by Deputy Attorney General Katzenbach, Brigadier General Henry Graham, and the federalized guard, Wallace stepped aside and the two students were registered.

The president spoke to the nation that night on television explaining that the use of troops had been required to enforce a federal court order for the admission of the students. He declared that:

We are confronted with a moral issue. It is as old as the scriptures and as clear as the American Constitution.

The heart of the question is whether all Americans are to be offered equal rights ane equal opportunities, whether we are going to treat our fellow citizens as we want to be treated. . . .[60]

For calling discrimination a moral issue, this address was hailed by some as the Second Emancipation Proclamation; by others it was called the Kennedy Manifesto.

On the public school front a trend toward an increased number of desegregated districts continued in 1963. Of the 161 districts desegregated in that year, only twenty were required by court order to be integrated. However, some of the remaining 141 did so because they were pressed by threatened litigation or by possible withdrawal of federal aid to impacted areas.[61]

New school desegregation in 1963 was accomplished without any serious disorder except in Birmingham, Alabama. There and at Tuskegee, Huntsville, and Mobile, Governor Wallace called out the state troopers to prevent the court-ordered desegregation of the schools. He ended his resistance on September 10 when the five federal district judges in Alabama enjoined him from further interference upon the request from the Justice Department, and after the president had called up the Alabama National Guard for federal duty.[62]

An evaluation of the Kennedy administration's achievements in education was made by Robert J. Steamer in 1963. He wrote that:

In appraising the Kennedy record on desegregation in education, one salient feature stands out: the President and his administration spokesmen have created a new mood which at the moment is primarily qualitative, but which will eventually have its quantitative effect on the Negro community. Following an era in which the federal executive had maintained a posture of an impartial agent of law enforcement and a neutral arbiter between Negro claims on the one hand and white supremacy on the other, the Kennedy Administration has resolutely moved the presidency into a position of support for the embattled judiciary on the side of Negro rights.[63]

Despite the gains made, however, much still needed to be done. There were some 3,053 public school districts in the southern and border states, and by the end of 1963, 1,141 had some degree of desegregation, much of it merely token. A little over one-third of the total number, in other words, had taken some steps at desegregating their schools.

## Employment

President Kennedy had made declarations during the campaign of 1960 about helping Negroes to obtain both government positions and government contract employment. The civil rights plank of the Democratic party platform had contained equally strong statements. The new president knew that not only were blacks under-employed in government and government contract work, but that they usually held the least skilled and lowest paid jobs in both. After a period of planning, the president made the following announcement on March 7, 1961:

I am today issuing an Executive Order combining the President's Committee on Government Contracts and the President's Committee on Government Employment Policy into a single President's Committee on Equal Employment Opportunity.

Through this vastly strengthened machinery I intend to ensure that Americans of all colors and beliefs will have equal access to employment within the government, and with those who do business with the government.

This order provides for centralization of responsibility for these policies under the Vice-President. It requires the Secretary of Labor—with all the resources of the Department of Labor at his command—to supervise the implementation of equal employment policies. And it grants, in specific terms, sanctions sweeping enough to ensure compliance.[64]

Along with Vice President Johnson as chairman of the Committee on Equal Employment Opportunity, the secretary of labor served as vice Chairman. In addition there were fourteen public members (including two Negroes) and ten cabinet level representatives, including Attorney General Kennedy.

In order to deal with the problem of discrimination in government employment each department or agency designated an official as Employment Policy Officer, who reported directly to his secretary or agency head. The Civil Service Commission sent special recruiters to Negro college campuses. This practice was also followed by some agencies and departments such as the Veterans' Administration, the Department of Labor, the Department of Commerce, the Department of State, and the FAA. Moreover, the Civil Service Commission held special meetings in regional centers in order to acquaint field managers and personnel officers with their responsibilities for eliminating job discrimination; and some government agencies such as the HHFA established intern programs for which Negro trainees were particularly sought.[65]

President Kennedy sent a letter to all federal employees on April 18, 1961, in which he directed that no association of federal employees practicing segregation or any kind of discrimination could use the sponsorship, name, or facilities of the government. The order had a special impact on employment recreational programs.[66] In another memorandum the president directed that the government would deal only with federal employee unions not practicing discrimination.[67] At least one government agency, the Atomic Energy Commission, and perhaps others, included the contractors under the president's directives.

The President's Committee on Equal Employment Opportunity made a report to the president on November 26, 1963. Concerning government employment it was pointed out that the agencies had lacked experienced personnel when the program was instituted. Therefore the committee undertook the training of top echelon employment policy officers and encouraged government agencies to establish their own training programs, and many did so.

In comparing federal employment as of June 1962, with June 1961, it was reported that:

The percentage of Negro federal employees in Grades 1-4 dropped from 72 percent to 69 percent while the number in the middle level, GS-5 positions through GS-11 positions climbed from 27 percent to 30 percent. Of the net increase of 62,633 jobs from June, 1961, to June, 1962, Negroes accounted for 10,737 or more than 17 percent.

—In Classification Act jobs, Negro employment in the middle

grades, GS-5 through GS-11, increased 19.2 percent compared with an overall increase of 2.4 percent, while in the upper grades, GS-12 through GS-18, the increase of Negroes was 35.8 percent compared with an overall increase of 9.5 percent.[68]

Only preliminary figures were available for 1963.

—Twenty-two percent of the net increase in Federal employment during the period represented increased Negro employment. This compares with 17 percent for the previous census period.

—This net increase brings the total reported Negro employment to a new high of 301,899—up 3 percent from 293,353 in June, 1962. The cumulative percentage increase from June, 1961, to June, 1963, amounted to 6.8 percent.

—There were 545 more Negroes in the grades GS-12 through GS-18 (paying $9,475 to $20,000) than there were a year earlier, an increase of 38.7 percent. The total number of jobs in these grades increased 12.4 percent during the same period.

—Negroes in the middle grades (GS-5—GS-11) increased by 4,278 or 14.7 percent, while total employment in these grades increased 5.1 percent.[69]

Despite the improvements Negroes were still largely concentrated in the lower positions in government employment. According to Alan B. Batchelder, in the range GS-12 to GS-18 (top grades), Negro employment increased 88 percent from 1961 to 1964, while for all groups the increase was 23 percent. Nevertheless he claimed that in 1964 only 1 percent of the employees in the top grades were Negroes.[70]

With regard to government contract employment, the president's executive order in 1961 required the inclusion of a nondiscrimination clause in all government contracts and the submission of periodic compliance reports by contractors and subcontractors to the contracting agency. The President's Committee on Equal Employment Opportunity had the authority to order a contracting agency to terminate a contract or refrain from entering into one with a potential contractor who had a record of noncompliance. The nondiscrimination clause also authorized the committee to declare a contractor who did not comply to be ineligible for additional government contracts. The committee could also require that a prospective contractor or subcontractor submit compliance reports concerned with previous contracts covered by the president's order. Reports as to the cooperation of labor unions and recommendations for securing cooperation were to be made periodically to President Kennedy.[71]

Less than a month after the committee began its operations Vice President Johnson called a meeting with presidents of fifty of the largest government contracting firms. The meeting took place on May 2, 1961, and Johnson obtained promises of cooperation and assistance from those firms in providing for equal job opportunity.[72] Most of these same firms later signed agreements under these so-called "Plans for Progress."

The procedure in developing a Plan for Progress called for discussion, study, and negotiation between the committee and a firm's management. After that there followed the execution of a final joint statement signed by the company's president and President Kennedy or Vice President Johnson. A constant effort was made to include companies not engaged in government contract work.

One year after the committee had come into existence, fifty-two companies had signed Plan for Progress agreements. By January 1963 the number had reached 104, and when the committee report was issued in November 1963, there were 115 (including several national concerns not holding government contracts) with a total of more than five and one-half million employees.[73]

A summary of reports from ninety-one companies was made available as of July 1963. The figures were slightly misleading because the companies joined the program at different times. Nine companies were filing their third report, thirty-two a second report, and it was the first time for fifty. Probably most of the "nonwhites" were Negroes.

Total employment in the 91 companies increased by 452,543 or 12.4 percent. Employment of nonwhites increased by 27,180 or 14.7 percent. Overall employment of all salaried employees (clerical to management) increased by only 13.8

percent. Nonwhite employment in these categories increased by 23.5 percent.

As of the initial reports of these companies there were 65.1 white salaried employees for each nonwhite. As of the latest reports of these companies, there were 60 white salaried employees for each nonwhite.[74]

As far as equal opportunities in organized labor were concerned, the 1963 report stated that although unions were not subject to sanctions, efforts were made to bring them into the program. On November 15, 1962, leaders of the AFL-CIO and 115 international union leaders signed Union Programs for Fair Practices with Vice President Johnson. The union leaders pledged to accelerate their unions' programs to ensure equal opportunity in union facilities and in all aspects of employment in which their unions were involved. The AFL-CIO established a Civil Rights Department to keep the committee informed on positive actions undertaken by unions.[75] Despite these actions little progress was made since many locals tended to ignore these arrangements.

In the meantime, on March 7, 1962, the President's Committee on Equal Employment Opportunity invoked the enforcement section of the Executive Order for the first time by publishing the names of two companies, which in consequence of their discriminatory practices, would no longer be eligible to receive future government contracts. On May 3, 1962, one of the two companies regained its eligibility.[76]

The Southern Regional Council made a study in Atlanta in early 1963 of twenty-four Plans for Progress firms. These firms had offices, plants, or regional headquarters in Atlanta. It was found that only three—Lockheed, Western Electric, and Goodyear—showed a vigorous desire to create equal job opportunities. Four others offered some evidence that they had tried to comply. On the other hand, a "few, in fact, didn't even know what the plans were: one regional manager called the program 'Alliance for Progress.' Others dismissed them out of hand. . . . Some felt they had done their part by hiring janitors. Some pleaded the pressure of local custom. . . ."[77]

*Newsweek* described the reaction in Washington to the Southern Regional Council report. One important individual saw comfort in that even three firms were complying with the Plans for Progress agreements. Others were dismayed that seventeen were not. The staff director of the U.S. Commission on Civil Rights, Berl Bernhard, found the report very disturbing. A Southern Regional Council member declared that there had been more publicity than progress in the program.[78]

Despite the weaknesses these programs were continued, and action was taken on other fronts in 1963. On June 22, 1963, President Kennedy issued Executive Order 11114 in which he extended the authority of the Committee on Equal Employment Opportunity to cover any federally assisted construction project, whether by loan, grant, contract, guaranty, or insurance; and he empowered the committee to withhold federal funds from any project in which discrimination against workers was practiced.[79]

At about the same time, the president directed Willard Wirtz, the secretary of labor, to require nondiscriminatory admission to programs coming under the Federal Apprenticeship Act. Furthermore, the Defense Department and other federal agencies increased their efforts to insure equal employment practices among the corporations with whom they negotiated governmental contracts.[80]

Harold Fleming in 1965 pointed out that the attempt to deal with discrimination in jobs under Executive Order 10925 (1961) had had little impact. He gave the following reasons: (1) there was little jurisdiction over labor unions; (2) automation had caused a decline in less skilled jobs, leaving the Negroes at a disadvantage; (3) a sense of high priority and presidential interest communicated to the contracting agencies soon diminished; (4) voluntary participation was inadequate; and (5) enforcement provisions were practically never used. In fact, "the ultimate sanction—contract termination—has never been applied, no hearings have been held, and only a few companies have been put on the list of ineligibles for future contracts pending improved performance."[81] Fleming concluded by pointing out that according to a Committee on Equal Employment Opportunity report in 1964, Negroes had increased since 1961 from 12.9 to 13.2 percent of all federal employees, and in 103 Plans for Progress companies the increase was from 5.1 to 5.7 percent.[82]

By the end of 1963 Negroes were still concentrated in the least skilled and poorest paying jobs in both public and private categories. Nevertheless Theodore Sorensen wrote concerning government contract work that even though no contracts were cancelled and the president and the attorney general were dissatisfied and skeptical of the glowing statistical reports of the committee, "major breakthroughs were made—in textile mills where Negroes had only been sweepers, in aircraft plants where they had been told not to apply, in thousands of new jobs and supervisory positions."[83]

The Kennedy administration had been involved on many fronts in dealing with the civil rights problem. Although some progress was achieved in all major areas, the administration obviously accomplished more in some than in others. Great efforts had been made, with varying degrees of success; and much remained to be done.

# 4. A Partial Case Study: The Drive for a Civil Rights Bill in 1963

The year 1963 witnessed a change in the president's legislative strategy. I will present a partial case study to show how President Kennedy used his various executive levers in an attempt to get a meaningful civil rights bill through Congress.

Originally, in 1961, President Kennedy had decided to stress executive action, and aside from the extension of the life of the Civil Rights Commission, the poll tax amendment, and the literacy test bill of 1962, no new legislation on civil rights had been proposed by the Kennedy administration. As Alexander Bickel wrote,

A first and obvious generalization is that the performance through 1962 was wholly executive. The administration broke no lances in Congress. As to this one need perhaps say no more than that President Kennedy was a realist, and he had troubles enough in what was in all intents and purposes a three-party legislature, with a species of Free Democrats (à la West Germany's) holding the balance of power. A second and more sweeping generalization, is that the performance was heavily a litigating one.[1]

But the way of litigation and, with it, negotiation, while useful, took a long time; and the demands of the blacks were increasing as many of them were speaking in terms of "Freedom Now." Moreover, the confrontation with Governor Ross Barnett of Mississippi over Meredith's entry into the university, reinforced by evidence of continued recalcitrance on the part of many southern white leaders, apparently moved Kennedy to change his strategy. Perhaps he was also encouraged by the recent Congressional elections in which the Republicans had gained but two seats at midterm, while the Democrats added four in the Senate. Though the conservative-liberal split remained in the House, there was at least a better chance of securing the necessary two-thirds vote to shut off a filibuster in the Senate.[2]

Interestingly enough, there was no indication of any change in the president's strategy to be found in his annual State of the Union message to Congress delivered on January 14, 1963. In fact he had little to say about civil rights in general and less still on that which pertained to the Negro. He declared: "And the most precious and powerful right in the world, the right to vote in a free American election, must not be denied to any citizen on grounds of his race or color. I wish that all qualified Americans permitted to vote were willing to vote, but surely in this centennial year of Emancipation all those who are willing to vote should always be permitted."[3]

Nevertheless, and seemingly with relatively little immediate outside pressure, President Kennedy resorted to one of his legislative levers when he made his first special message to Congress on civil rights a little over a month later on February 28, 1963. He stated:

> In the last two years, more progress has been made in securing the civil rights of all Americans than in any comparable period of our history. Progress has been made—through executive action, litigation, persuasion and private initiative —in achieving and protecting equality of opportunity in education, voting, transportation, employment, housing, government, and the enjoyment of public accommodations.
>
> But pride in our accomplishments must not give way to relaxation of our effort. Nor does progress in the Executive Branch enable the Legislative Branch to escape its own obligations. On the contrary, it is in the belief that Congress will wish again to meet its responsibilities in this matter, that I stress in the following agenda of existing and prospective action important legislative as well as administrative measures.[4]

In the area of voting he pointed out that in a recent survey of five states less than fifteen percent of the Negroes of voting age were registered to vote. The president did not name the five states, but according to the Justice Department they were Alabama, Louisiana, Georgia, Mississippi, and South Carolina. To remedy the situation, he proposed that federal referees be empowered to place Negroes on the registration rolls while litigation was pending. With regard to litigation the president recommended a law providing that voting suits would be expedited and judged ahead of other types of suits in federal courts. Moreover, he requested a bill that prohibited the application of different tests, standards, procedures, or practices for different applicants who sought to register and to vote in federal elections. He then repeated his proposal made in 1962 that a sixth-grade education would constitute a presumption of literacy in federal elections.[5]

At the same time the president complained about the slow pace of desegregation in the southern schools. In order to speed up the development he recommended a program of federal technical assistance to help school districts while in the process of desegregation. Finally Kennedy proposed that the life of the Civil Rights Commission be extended by at least four more years and that the commission be authorized to serve as a national civil rights clearing house providing advice, information, and technical assistance to any private or public agency requesting its services.[6]

Although the president's proposals for new legislation did demonstrate a stronger conviction on the part of the administration to aid the Negroes, both the Negro leaders and the Civil Rights Commission were nevertheless bitterly disappointed at their mildness. Both the commission and the Negro leaders communicated this attitude to the White House. They were dismayed, for example, that nothing was really provided to hasten the process of school desegregation, to combat discrimination in employment and housing, and to ensure equal access to public accommodations. The president remained unshaken in his belief that nothing more could be accomplished at the time.

Senator Philip Hart of Michigan and a number of colleagues prepared a bill incorporating the administration's proposals dealing with the Civil Rights Commission. Other congressmen, including Representative Emanuel Celler of New York, drew up bills which contained the other Kennedy proposals. Congressional committees in both houses held hearings throughout the spring of 1963, but no real progress was in sight. While Congress pursued its leisurely pace, the civil rights movement was gaining a new momentum.

The Civil Rights Commission made an important contribution to the new sense of urgency. The commission was distressed over several efforts made by the attorney general to postpone a session in Mississippi to look into the miserable conditions there and dramatize them. In addition, the commission was intent on showing how inadequate the president's legislative program was to deal with segregation. On April 16, 1963, an interim report based on investigations by the Advisory Commission in Mississippi was issued to the public. Among other things the members recommended that the president and Congress should consider cutting off federal funds from Mississippi until that state ended its subversion of the Constitution and federal laws. The commission pointed out that in the fiscal year 1962 the state had paid $270 million in federal taxes, while it had received $650 million in return from the federal government regardless of the discriminatory expenditure of those funds. The FAA, it was pointed out, had granted $2.1 million for a jet airport in Jackson, Mississippi, without questioning local plans to segregate terminal restaurants and rest rooms.'

The commission's disclosures about conditions in Mississippi were notable for their shock effects. For example:

In angry language the commission reported how Negroes seeking to register to vote in Mississippi had been "shot, set upon by police dogs, beaten, and otherwise terrorized." Worse still, in the commission's eyes, Leflore County had at the height of a registration drive—cut off Federal surplus-food allotments to 17,000 needy recipients, most of them Negroes and some of them "Children at the brink of starvation."[8]

As to the effect of this report, as Foster Rhea Dulles pointed out: "Nothing could have more clearly demonstrated the inadequacy of existing civil rights legislation. Whatever else may be said of the Mississippi Report, it helped shatter any existing complacency over progress in the South. It drove home the imperative need for further Congressional moves if the Negroes were in fact to win the right to vote and otherwise enjoy equality before the law."[9]

In the meantime the Negroes of Birmingham launched a drive under the leadership of Martin Luther King, Jr., to end discrimination in shops, restaurants, and employment. This effort met determined resistance from city authorities resulting in injunctions and numerous arrests. The leading figure among the authorities was T. Eugene "Bull" Connor, the police commissioner. King was arrested along with Ralph Abernathy and fifty-three others. Many other arrests (including hundreds of school children) followed, and the police used fire hoses and police dogs. Mrs. King, who was convalescing after bearing her fourth child, became worried about her husband after not hearing from him and called Robert Kennedy to see what could be done. Later she received a call from the president, and he assured her that a check would be made concerning her husband's safety.[10] The check was conducted, and his safety reported to Mrs. King. Shortly thereafter King was released when an unknown person posted his bail.

Both incensed and alarmed, the president and the attorney general sent Burke Marshall to negotiate with leaders on both sides of the controversy in Birmingham. Meanwhile, in Washington, Robert Kennedy, Secretary of Defense McNamara, and Secretary of Treasury Dillon made many telephone calls to influential businessmen and industrialists, pressing for quick settlement. Moreover, Eugene Rostow, dean of the Yale Law School, volunteered his services and contacted Roger Blough, chairman of U. S. Steel, who was a Yale law school graduate. In turn Blough called on his Birmingham associates and urged on them the importance of reaching a settlement. A truce was arranged quickly.[11] At a news conference on May 8 President Kennedy announced his satisfaction over the progress made there.[12] It did not last long, however.

Bull Connor had in the meanwhile sent for aid from Governor Wallace, who dispatched several hundred state troopers. The truce was destroyed as Wallace made inflammatory remarks and white extremists bombed houses and hotels in the Negro districts, including the home of A. D. King, a brother of Martin Luther King, Jr. More violence followed, and on May 12 President Kennedy broadcast a nationwide speech, urging calm. He pointed out that the earlier truce agreement was fair and just. He announced that he was sending Marshall back, alerting Air Force units trained in riot control to be sent to bases near Birmingham, and taking preliminary steps to federalize the Alabama National Guard.[13] Governor Wallace then threatened to send in more state troopers to put down black demonstrations. President Kennedy warned him by telegram on May 13 not to do so and reminded him of the preliminary steps already taken the day before.[14] Things gradually settled down, and apparently the president's stand persuaded the Birmingham authorities to use more equitable measures in upholding law and order.

Other incidents occurred which brought more attention to the Negroes' plight. A white postman, William L. Moore, upset over the treatment of Negroes, made a protest march from Tennessee to Alabama, and he was murdered in northeastern Alabama. There was also the University of Alabama episode that fizzled out with Wallace's symbolic blockade at the door. Medgar Evers, NAACP leader in Mississippi, was murdered early in June 1963. Furthermore, demonstrations and riots took place in such cities as Greensboro, North Carolina; Albany, Georgia; Selma, Alabama; Nashville, Tennessee; and many others.

The president and the nation were awakened by these incidents, but Americans had been most profoundly shocked by the television and newspaper photographs of the brutal tactics of the Birmingham police. Theodore Sorensen wrote that:

"The civil rights movement," the President often said thereafter, "should thank God for Bull Connor. He's helped it as much as Abraham Lincoln." But news photographers deserve a share of the credit. Front-page pictures of Connor's police dogs savagely attacking Negroes, of fire hoses pounding them against the street, of burly policemen sitting on a female demonstrator, aroused the nation and the world. Previously timid Negroes were spurred into action in their own cities. Previously indifferent whites were shocked into sympathy. And President John Fitzgerald Kennedy, recognizing that the American conscience was at last beginning to stir, began laying down his own plans for awakening that conscience to the need for further action.[15]

The day after the worst incidents in Birmingham there appeared a photograph in the newspapers showing a police dog lunging at a

Negro woman. The president told a group from the Americans for Democratic Action that the picture had made him sick.[16] It also profoundly affected Robert Kennedy.[17]

Shortly thereafter President Kennedy made a trip to Tennessee and Alabama, at which time he saluted the ninetieth anniversary of Vanderbilt University and the thirtieth anniversary of the Tennessee Valley Authority. During his speeches the president reminded his listeners of their rights and responsibilities as American citizens. At Muscle Shoals, in the presence of Governor Wallace, he cited the TVA and other popular federal programs to demonstrate that the federal government was not just an adversary or an intruder. He declared that in favoring the building of the TVA, Senator Norris and President Roosevelt had not been fearful of directing the power and purpose of the nation toward a solution of national problems. Sorensen noted that even "Governor Wallace could not have missed the meaning."[18]

The White House and the Justice Department then began to prepare a new series of legislative proposals. The president decided to go ahead with a sweeping new bill on May 31, over the opposition of some of his political advisers who foresaw both congressional and electoral defeat.[19] He also decided on June 11 to make public his greater commitment to the cause of civil rights. In his nationally televised address the president referred to the injustices suffered by Negro citizens. He pointed out that "[t]his is not even a legal or legislative issue alone. It is better to settle these matters in the courts than on the streets, and new laws are needed at every level, but law alone cannot make men see right."[20] In this same speech Kennedy called the racial crisis a moral issue.

Then the President declared that the following week he was going to ask Congress to act on the proposition that race had no place in American life or law. He pointed out that already the judiciary and the executive branches of government had made that commitment and that it was time for Congress to act. He would ask Congress to enact legislation on the following: (1) to give all Americans the right to have facilities opened to the public—restaurants, hotels, retail stores, theaters, and similar establishments; (2) to authorize the federal government to participate more fully in lawsuits concerned with ending segregation in public education;

and (3) other features would be included in the requests, including greater participation by the federal government in protecting the right to vote.[21]

Richard Neustadt perhaps best summed up the president's decision when he wrote that:

Thereby he undertook an irrevocable commitment to Negro integration in American society, aiming once again to get through the effort with society intact. He evidently came to see the risks of social escalation, and he sought to steer a course toward integration which could hold inside our social order both impatient Negroes and reactive whites—as tough a task of politics as we have known, and one he faced no sooner than he had to. But he faced it. What Vienna, Berlin, and Cuba were to his first purpose,[22] Oxford, and then Birmingham were to his second purpose; events which shaped his personal commitment.[23]

A leading civil rights spokesman, Howard Zinn, had this to say about the new Kennedy commitment:

That the pressure of world opinion, and the obvious power of Negro sentiment in this country, were the key factors in producing this change, should not detract from the praise due the national administration for its sensitivity in reacting as it did. But the argument is reinforced, that the Negro is still not, in himself, a number one priority as a human problem. He must wait for considerations of politics and pressure to move the nation into giving him another lift on his way to full freedom.[24]

In the meantime, prior to the submission of the new program to Congress, administration spokesmen explained to members of the Leadership Conference on Civil Rights that they were not planning to cover all public accommodations in the new measure and were thinking of applying Part III—Desegregation of Public Facilities—only to school desegregation. The civil rights groups and their allies on Capitol Hill pressed for a much broader program, including a fair employment title, a complete Part III, total coverage of public accommodations, a clause forbidding federal aid to all activities practicing segregation, and federal administrative procedures for the registration of voters. Members of the

Democratic Study Group wired the president that his program was inadequate.[25]

But the president, though determined to move ahead, had to consider the fate of his tax reduction bill and the rest of his program. For the most part the counsel of caution prevailed, as was clear when the Kennedy program was presented to Congress on June 19, 1963. In his message Kennedy mentioned at the outset that his requests of February 28 had not been acted upon as yet. At the same time he stressed that the Negroes' drive for justice had not remained stationary nor would it do so until full equality had been achieved. Indeed, he continued,

. . . (t)he growing and understandable dissatisfaction of Negro citizens with the present pace of desegregation and their increased determination to secure for themselves the equality of opportunity and treatment to which they are rightfully entitled, have underscored what should have already been clear: the necessity of the Congress enacting this year—not only the measures already proposed—but also additional legislation providing legal remedies for the denial of certain individual rights.[26]

Kennedy proposed that Congress remain in session until the legislation was enacted, and he stated a preference for a single omnibus bill. The bill would include provisions dealing with: (1) an extension of the life of the Civil Rights Commission and an expansion of its duties, (2) voting rights, (3) equal accommodations, (4) employment, (5) federally assisted programs, (6) a Community Relations Service, and (7) education. Moreover, he requested legislative and budgetary amendments to "improve the training, skills and economic opportunities of the economically distressed and discontented, white and Negro alike."[27]

In order to obtain the enactment of the program the president realized that he had to appeal beyond Congress, and this would be even more necessary in order to persuade the American people to accept the new law. Therefore the president, joined by Vice President Johnson and Robert Kennedy, involved himself in numerous meetings at the White House in which he sought to obtain the cooperation of over 1,600 national leaders: southern leaders, Negro leaders, educators, mayors, women's groups, lawyers, business organizations, governors, editors—segregationists as well as integrationists. The three men briefed these groups not only on the bill but also on their responsibilities after the bill became law. Here was an example of presidential leadership.[28]

President Kennedy and Vice President Johnson took special pains in conferring with the spokesmen of the Leadership Conference on Civil Rights. They explained that the balance of power in the Senate was held by senators from the western and mountain states where civil rights was not a burning issue and that all might be lost if too much were requested. It was, nevertheless, agreed that the civil rights groups would point out imperfections and seek to strengthen the bills in Congress.[29]

The president also pressed the leaders of the labor movement for support. Some of them had long given lip service to civil rights; but in reality Negroes had been excluded from craft unions, Negroes had been forced into situations where there were segregated locals and seniority systems, and Negroes had been denied required apprenticeship training. The president asked that such policies of discrimination be discontinued. Moreover, he gave special attention to clergymen of all faiths and to the blue ribbon Business Council.[30]

After the president's proposals were delivered to Congress, the Senate Judiciary Committee, under the chairmanship of James Eastland, held hearings but took no action. The Senate Commerce Committee, to which the public accommodations section had been referred as a separate measure, approved a bill on October 8 which incorporated the president's proposal. For reasons of strategy, however, it was decided not to make a formal report in 1963, since the bill could be called up and subjected to a filibuster before the House acted, and thus the entire effort would be undermined.

The House then proved to be the crucial body since Celler's Judiciary Committee provided a favorable forum. In the House as a whole, because of a division between southern and nonsouthern Democrats, the balance of power belonged to the Republicans— particularly under the leadership of Minority Leader Charles Halleck and William McCulloch, ranking Republicans on the Judiciary Committee. Not unexpectedly, the administration decided to cultivate the Republicans.

Meanwhile the Leadership Conference on Civil Rights bore down on the House Judiciary Committee. On August 28 a giant and peaceful rally was held in Washington, D.C., with several hundred thousand participants. The demonstrators called attention to Negro demands for immediate equality in employment and in other areas of civil rights as well.

To handle the civil rights bill, Chairman Emanuel Celler used his Subcommittee No. 5, the Antitrust Committee. This group was favorably disposed toward civil rights and had none of the full committee's senior southerners on it. By the end of September the subcommittee had gone beyond the administration's proposals. It approved a bill which embodied nearly all of the Leadership Conrerence's demands—a complete Part III (Desegregation of Public Facilities), a fair employment practices section, extension of voting rights protection to include state as well as federal elections, extension of the public accommodations section to all state-licensed businesses, and a mandatory cut-off of federal funds to any activities practicing discrimination. The new version of the bill was then taken before the entire Judiciary Committee, and the southerners rallied to its support in the hope that it would be regarded as too extreme and thus would be defeated in the full House.

The administration became thoroughly alarmed and fearful that no bill at all would be passed. Behind the scenes negotiations were begun between the attorney general and Halleck and McCulloch. Moreover, Attorney General Kennedy appeared before the Judiciary Committee to speak in favor of weakening the subcommittee's measure. He insisted that the subcommittee's bill had some provisions that were either unwise or would provoke unnecessary opposition. He was equally critical of the public accommodations section and the new Title II, which would have given the Justice Department almost unlimited powers in filing suits to stop deprivations of civil rights. After presenting these critical remarks, Robert Kennedy outlined a compromise which he argued should be accepted. Furthermore, he insisted as a practical matter that only a compromise had a chance of passage in Congress.[31]

The following day the attorney general appeared again before the committee to answer questions. Celler, the chairman of the Judiciary Committee who had been largely responsible for writing the stronger bill, made a strategic retreat. He was willing to accept a compromise in order to obtain Republican support.[32] William McCulloch was also impressed by the attorney general's appearances before the committee.[33]

Despite Robert Kennedy's efforts, however, most of the liberal Democrats on the committee were adamant in their support of the subcommittee's bill. They were suspicious that the Republicans might outmaneuver them. At this point the attorney general advised the president that only his direct and immediate intervention would prevent passage of the subcommittee's bill which both of them felt was surely doomed and would be voted down in the House.

A series of White House meetings were held in which the president talked with key members of the Judiciary Committee, such as Celler and McCulloch, and with other House leaders including Speaker McCormack, Carl Albert, the majority leader, Charles Halleck, and Leslie Arends, the minority whip. The President also held frequent telephone conversations with other members of the Judiciary Committee. In order to win over some of the liberal Democrats the President found that he had to obtain a commitment from House Republican leaders to support a compromise through the committee, the Rules Committee, and on the House floor. Before making such a commitment, the Republicans in turn demanded that the president gain sufficient Democratic support for the bill all the way through the House. In addition, the Republicans requested modifications in the bill such as the following: (1) dropping of the provision for a temporary voting registrar formula for special three-judge federal courts; (2) removal of the provision for making the Civil Rights Commission permanent; (3) elimination of the Community Relations Service; (4) the addition of a fair employment section with court instead of administrative enforcement of decisions; and (5) a modification of Title III. The president accepted these changes.[34] A bill incorporating the necessary amendments was prepared by Katzenbach and Marshall in cooperation with Republican staff members. A pact was concluded between the president and Minority Leader Halleck on the day of the committee vote which called for joint cooperation without acceptance of amendments through final voting in the House.

As a result of the agreement between the administration and the Republican leaders, the subcommittee's bill was voted down, and the bipartisan measure supported by the administration was approved.[35] As it was reported out of the committee the new bill was stronger than that originally proposed by the president in that it contained a fair employment practices title. Moreover, Part III had been broadened in its coverage. On the other hand, the voting rights provision had been weakened.[36] The Civil Rights Commission was not mentioned. In fact, the life of that body was merely extended for one year in separate action by both houses. No new power was given to the Civil Rights Commission.

Robert Kennedy termed the new compromise measure a better bill than the original one proposed by the administration.[37] President Kennedy issued the following statement on the day of the Judiciary Committee approval:

The House Committee on the Judiciary, in approving a bipartisan civil rights bill today, has significantly improved the prospects for the enactment of effective civil rights legislation in Congress this year. The bill is a comprehensive and fair bill.

From the very beginning, enactment of an effective civil rights bill has required that sectional and political differences be set aside in the interest of meeting an urgent national crisis. The action by the committee today reflects this kind of leadership by the Speaker of the House, John McCormack, House Minority Leader, Charles Halleck, Committee Chairman, Emanuel Celler, and the ranking Minority Member, William McCulloch.[38]

The compromise bill had just reached the House Rules Committee when the president left on his ill-fated journey to Dallas.[39] He had paid a price for his stronger stand on civil rights, even though some liberals and civil rights leaders did not think he had gone far enough. In many parts of the South the feelings of the whites toward John Kennedy had reached a point of incredibly bitter hatred. Furthermore a reaction had developed in the northern states against Negro demonstrations and demands. In the fall of 1963 municipal elections were held in Philadelphia, Detroit, Chicago, and Cleveland; and the results indicated enough defections among ordinary white voters against the Democrats to imperil the president's chance of being re-elected in 1964.[40]

The president was not blind to these developments, but he had decided to take a stand. Indeed he still thought that he might win in 1964, even with southern white hostility and the backlash among ordinary white voters in the North.

The president's leadership role had been vital in obtaining a meaningful bill which had a chance of passage in the House. His goal of enacting a civil rights bill was unfulfilled because of his death on November 22, 1963. But a new president, Lyndon Johnson, made it plain in an address to Congress a few days later that he meant to see the bill passed into law. His own leadership played a major role in fulfilling that part of John F. Kennedy's program by July 1964, when the most far-reaching civil rights bill in American history became law. A significant step had been taken toward making the Negro a first-class citizen in the United States.

# 5. Epilogue

The one-thousand days of John F. Kennedy as president witnessed some significant efforts to make progress on the civil rights front. Unlike his predecessor, Dwight Eisenhower, Kennedy had placed himself at the head of the civil rights movement by the time of his death.

Various commentators have argued as to whether or not his commitment to civil rights was "passionate," and some writers insist that Kennedy did not have a large degree of commitment at first, even if he did have later. To this writer, at least, his being passionate or not is not so important as what he actually did while he held office. After all, external signs of passion may be merely a matter of style. And in making an attempt at evaluation, it is well to bear in mind that any president of the United States is constantly confronted with manifold problems demanding his time. Of necessity he must give priority to those matters that seem the most urgent at the moment. It is very difficult for the president to give top priority to any one area very long, particularly on the domestic front, when there are always many others demanding his attention. In the general area of foreign affairs alone where the president's voice is pre-eminent, he is indeed a man who must very carefully guard his time.

There is another dimension on this matter of the presidency, and that is the president must carefully guard not only his time but also whatever power and influence he possesses. The supply of these essential elements is not limitless. And, perhaps as Richard E. Neustadt has indicated, the most important of the instruments he has at his command is his ability to persuade others to do certain things they would not otherwise do. He can do this in large part because of his prestige and his willingness at times, if necessary, to use some of the levers he has at his disposal. Undoubtedly he can furnish, above all, moral leadership. But he is limited as to how often he may attempt to exercise this leadership, and to a great extent the time must be propitious. Certainly, if he tries a "fireside" chat or national television appeal too often, he loses his effect. By the same token, if he undertakes much more than he can deliver by way of a program, he may disappoint those who expect much, and he may lose his standing with those he wishes to help as well as infuriate others who oppose changes.

All this should be kept in mind when one attempts to appraise the overall accomplishments of the Kennedy administration in the field of civil rights. It is true that the Democratic party platform and the president promised more than could be delivered in a few years. Nevertheless it is well to remember that John Kennedy emphasized the use of executive power more than anything else during the heat of the campaign. Given the outcome of the election in which he won by a little over 100,000 votes and returns from the congressional elections, it is little wonder that he decided to rely on executive power and not to request additional legislation for awhile. The primary methods employed in 1961 and 1962 were litigation and negotiation. Of course, when confronted with defiance of the federal court at the University of Mississippi in 1962, after efforts at conciliation proved unfruitful, he made use of force just as President Eisenhower had finally done in Little Rock in 1957.

President Kennedy did make two legislative proposals in 1962: the abolition of the poll tax for federal primaries and elections and the substitution of a sixth-grade education for the literacy test for voting. Only the anti-poll tax amendment was adopted. The year 1963 proved to be different, however. Seeing that some progress had been made through the use of executive power, but not enough, Kennedy threw down the gauntlet and made stronger legislative proposals. These proved to be too mild. The cause was aided by the report on Mississippi by the Civil Rights Commission and, above all, by the abuses from which the blacks suffered in Birmingham. By the time of his death in November 1963, an even stronger civil rights bill was on its way through Congress. His major levers in pressing for the bill had been messages to Congress, public speeches and television appeals, and private negotiations with interest groups and congressional leaders.

In looking at the special areas of discrimination that have been emphasized in this study, let me mention the major executive tools and attempt a brief appraisal as to the effectiveness of each program. In appointing Negroes to important posts in government, President Kennedy was in part, at least, paying a political debt for support given to him during the election by blacks. He took the precaution of naming to high posts those who were eminently qualified for them. Moreover, the president set the tone for American society as a whole by discouraging administrative officials from engaging in discriminatory activities even on the social plane. Most high officials complied with his views in this respect. It would be difficult to say how much impact this effort had outside government.

The greatest success took place in the field of interstate transportation. By the ICC order, litigation, and negotiation, segregation was all but eliminated during the Kennedy administration. The president's major personal efforts stemmed from his request to the attorney general that a petition be sent to the ICC and from his public statement in which he upheld the right to travel in interstate commerce.

The Kennedy administration continued the efforts made by the Truman and Eisenhower administrations to end discrimination in the armed forces. Although discrimination had been lessened on the bases, still too high a percentage of Negroes was to be found in the lower ranks at both the enlisted and officer level. The report issued by the President's Committee on Equal Opportunity in the Armed Forces pointed the way for significant reforms. Some important changes were inaugurated by the Department of Defense in response to the committee's report and to prodding by the president. The base commander was given major responsibilities for dealing with off-base discrimination. Furthermore, administrative machinery was established within the Department of Defense to deal with segregation and its eradication. Finally, the reserve establishment was integrated during the Kennedy administration, but not the National Guard. In dealing with this area, then, the president had utilized, above all, an executive order creating the Gesell

Committee, and afterwards he encouraged the Defense Department to issue directives in an effort to carry out the committee's recommendations.

In the field of public housing the most significant action was the president's "stroke of the pen" in November 1962. That action, though promised in 1960 during the election campaign, was delayed—apparently for political reasons. In addition, when the president issued the executive order it was not nearly as far-reaching in its import as had been anticipated. Only a relatively small percentage of housing was directly affected. Even so, a precedent was set for stronger action later on. The executive order of 1962 was the major lever used by the president in regard to housing.

Education also witnessed some progress toward desegregation. In this field the administration was hampered by the lack of legislation and the nature of the federal system. Nevertheless, the president and the attorney general affirmed their support of the school desegregation cases and efforts were made by the Justice Department through litigation and negotiation to bring about desegregation of the public schools. Some attempts were made to deal with discrimination in impacted area schools, but no federal funds were withdrawn because of segregation in the public schools. In the face of defiance of the court, of course, the administration called out the National Guard and dispatched federal marshals to ensure the enrollment of James Meredith at the University of Mississippi. There was not as much trouble when it came to the registration of two black students at the University of Alabama, though Governor Wallace made a gesture of resistance and President Kennedy federalized the Alabama National Guard. By the time of President Kennedy's death there was some degree of desegregation of public educational institutions in all fifty states. However, in terms of the overall picture, there was still a long way to go before achieving full desegregation of public schools. In education the major tools of the president were public pronouncements, the issuance of executive orders calling out federal forces to enforce court decrees, litigation and threats of litigation, and private persuasion.

In the field of voting the Department of Justice engaged in a great deal of litigation. This was indeed a slow process, since it took a long time for a case to be prepared and completed. In addition, as in other fields, there was a need for additional legislation as the president determined in 1962. More drastic reforms were urged in 1963. Nevertheless, though many Negroes still could not register and vote in 1963, many more could than in 1961 both as a result of suits and cooperation between the Justice Department and the Voter Education Project as a result of which Negroes were encouraged to register and to vote. By 1963 Negroes were becoming a political force in the South, particularly in the metropolitan areas, and they were registered to vote in some counties where either none or only a few had voted before. The major tools used in voting were litigation and investigation by the Justice Department, encouragement of Negro voting, presidential messages to the public and Congress, and presidential requests for additional legislation.

The field of employment proved perhaps the most difficult to undertake. The major tools were executive orders, presidential speeches, private exhortation, negotiations, threats of sanctions, and emphasis on the hiring of qualified Negroes in the civil service. By executive order President Kennedy merged the two committees dealing with government and government contract employment and called the new organization the President's Committee on Equal Employment Opportunity, under the chairmanship of Vice President Johnson. In addition a strong effort was made to hire blacks in government employment, at least for a time. Special administrative machinery was established in governmental agencies to eliminate discrimination and to improve the Negroes' opportunities for advancement. Moreover, many of the governmental agencies sponsored internship programs which trained Negroes for employment in government. By 1963 though there had been a slight improvement in the total number of Negroes hired by the government and some at the higher GS levels; nevertheless Negroes were still largely located at the lower GS levels. Very few Negroes were employed at the GS-12 to GS-18 range.

In government contract employment "Plans for Progress" agreements were made with a large number of firms to ban discrimination in their employment policies. There were sanctions, including withdrawal of the contract in the event of noncompliance, but they were hardly used and withdrawal of a contract never occurred.

Moreover, a large number of American firms were not covered since they did not hold government contracts, though a few such firms voluntarily joined in the "Plans for Progress" programs. President Kennedy issued another executive order in 1963 extending the authority of the Committee on Equal Employment Opportunity to cover federally assisted construction projects.

Overall, however, not many more Negroes were hired by governmental contract firms than before the program was instituted. Furthermore, the Negroes tended to hold the more menial jobs and relatively few important executive positions with the "Plans for Progress" firms. An added problem, of course, was that labor unions frequently discriminated against Negroes, and although many of the leaders at the top of labor entered into agreements with the Committee on Equal Employment Opportunity to try to ban discriminatory practices, there was still much discrimination practiced by the local unions. No real sanctions existed to deal with this problem.

In comparing the Kennedy Administration with those of Roosevelt, Truman, and Eisenhower, there can be no doubt that much more was accomplished on the civil rights front during the one thousand days that John F. Kennedy held the presidency. One could argue persuasively that there was little real perception of the plight of the Negro as a special problem during most of the Roosevelt Administration. As already noted, the Negroes did benefit as others did among the poor from the actions of the New Deal in coping with the depression. The emphasis was on their being poor rather than the color of their skin. No real effort was made to break the barriers that surrounded the Negroes at every turn.

In World War II a breakthrough was accomplished with the establishment of the FEPC for government contract employment. At the same time there was little change in the segregated patterns of the armed services or in the rest of American life. Toward the end of the war, following the death of President Roosevelt, Harry Truman became the president. He initiated desegregation in the armed forces and called for what then seemed to be a very far-reaching legislative program dealing with civil rights. President Truman also set up a Fair Employment Practices Board in the Civil Service Commission to replace the FEPC which had been discontinued by Congress. Though none of his legislative program was enacted into law, President Truman established many precedents for later presidents to follow.

President Eisenhower continued efforts toward desegregation of the armed forces, promoted desegregation in Washington, and established committees to deal with discrimination in both government and government contract employment. In general, however, he held a Whig view of the presidency, and he disliked the use of executive power to right what he regarded as basically local problems. He never committed himself publicly when it came to the school desegregation cases, and this lack of approval made him appear to be at least neutral on civil rights matters. Despite his "negativism," however, and after much procrastination, President Eisenhower set an important precedent when he sent in federal troops to enforce a federal court order which called for school desegregation in Little Rock.

The 1960 campaign provided a consensus between the two parties and Presidential candidates on the need for major governmental actions on civil rights. John F. Kennedy emphasized that he would chiefly utilize executive instruments during the campaign. Given the closeness of the election and the situation in Congress, the new president proceeded to rely on executive powers to improve the situation for the Negro. Almost immediately, he took the step Eisenhower had refused to take when he declared publicly his support for the *Brown* decision of 1954. The year 1963 proved to be a turning point for President Kennedy as he came to realize that change was not proceeding rapidly enough in civil rights. In that year he placed himself at the head of the civil rights movement and publicly attacked racial discrimination as being morally wrong. Undoubtedly the shocking events at Birmingham hastened his change of attitude and policy. Following his commitment the president decided to seek more far-reaching legislation, though he remained a pragmatist who did not wish to propose a program that could not be adopted in Congress and thus not only make enemies of those opposed to more reform, but also those whose expectations would be blunted. At the time of his death in November 1963 the Civil Rights Bill had reached the House Rules Committee where its fate was unknown.

Unquestionably the time had come to take rather drastic action in 1963. President Kennedy did not seek to push too far ahead of the American people on civil rights; but he did go far enough to embitter not only many of the whites in the South but also many in the North as well. He did not shrink from what he regarded as his responsibilities when the time had arrived to make changes in order to maintain the fabric of American society. And he used effectively those tools available to all Presidents: (1) issued administrative and executive orders; (2) made public appeals through the mass media; (3) attempted to persuade government officials to follow certain policies; (4) made private contact with important persons outside of government in order to influence their actions; (5) called conferences to influence interest groups and Congressmen; (6) made proposals to Congress; (7) named committees to investigate certain issues and supported their recommendations; (8) threatened use of the purse strings; (9) made appointments of outstanding Negroes to significant government posts; (10) appointed whites to important posts who were sensitive to Negro demands; (11) discouraged federal officials from attending segregated gatherings; (12) used force and threat of force to support court decrees; and (13) used his authority as commander-in-chief to make changes in the armed services and the communities where they served.

President Kennedy changed the image of the presidency from a position of seeming neutrality on civil rights as under Eisenhower to one of positive actions on behalf of the frustrated blacks. In his executive actions, President Kennedy relied heavily on precedents established during previous administrations, particularly that of President Truman. In fact, one might say that Kennedy returned the presidency to the attempt at leadership of the civil rights movement as under Truman. John F. Kennedy was, of course, more successful, though much remained to be done at the time of his death.

# Notes

## Notes for Chapter 1

1. Harold C. Fleming, "The Federal Executive and Civil Rights: 1961-1965," *Daedelus*, 94 (1965), 923.
2. Richard J. Stillman II, *Integration of the Negro in the U. S. Armed Forces* (New York, 1968), pp. 41-42.
3. James L. Sundquist, *Politics and Policy* (Washington, 1968), pp. 223-224.
4. According to a member of his staff, the president stated to him privately that "I am convinced that the Supreme Court decision set back progress in the South at least fifteen years." See Emmet John Hughes, *The Ordeal of Power* (New York, 1963), p. 201.
5. *The White House Years* (Garden City, 1965), p. 150. See also Alexander M. Bickel, *Politics and the Warren Court* (New York, 1965), p. 51.
6. Robert J. Streamer, "Presidential Stimulus and School Desegregation," *Phylon,* 24 (Spring 1963), 21.
7. Owen Birnbaum, "Equal Employment Opportunity and Executive Order 10925," *University of Kansas Law Review,* 11 (October 1962), 18-19.

## Notes for Chapter 2

1. Clifford M. Lytle, "The History of the Civil Rights Bill of 1964," *Journal of Negro History,* 51 (1966), 282.

2. Sundquist, *Politics and Policy,* pp. 251-252. See also "Civil Rights Planks in the Party Platforms," *Current History,* 39 (1960), 237-240.

3. John F. Kennedy's Acceptance Speech, July 15, 1960, *Congressional Digest,* 39 (1960), 253.

4. Ibid., p. 255.

5. Theodore H. White, *The Making of the President 1960* (New York, 1962), pp. 256-258.

6. Sundquist, *Politics and Policy,* p. 253. See also "Civil Rights in the Party Platform," pp. 237, 240, 244.

7. "Nixon: The Goals of a New Administration," *U. S. News & World Report,* 49 (August 8, 1960), 96.

8. Ibid., p. 98.

9. "Civil Rights," *Congressional Quarterly Weekly Report,* 18 (August 12, 1960), 1434.

10. Arthur M. Schlesinger, Jr., *A Thousand Days* (Boston, 1965), p. 929.

11. "Civil Rights Pledges Trouble Kennedy Administration," *Congressional Quarterly Weekly Report,* 19 (April 21, 1961), 667.

12. Sundquist, *Politics and Policy,* p. 254; Bickel, *Politics and the Warren Court,* p. 49; and Schlesinger, *A Thousand Days,* p. 929.

13. "Civil Rights: The Kennedy Record," *New Republic,* 147 (December 15, 1962), 11.

14. White, *The Making of the President 1960,* pp. 321-323, and Theodore C. Sorensen, *Kennedy* (New York, 1965), p. 188.

15. Sorensen, *Kennedy,* pp. 340-342.

16. See the *Congressional Quarterly Almanac 1961,* XVII (Washington, D. C., 1961), 402.

17. "Equal Now," *Nation,* 192 (February 4, 1961), 91-95. See also Sorensen, *Kennedy,* p. 476, and Louis W. Koenig, *The Chief Executive* (New York, 1964), p. 327.

18. *The Federal Executive and Civil Rights* (Atlanta, 1961), p. 1.

19. Ibid., p. 2.

20. Ibid., p. 48.

21. Sorensen, *Kennedy,* p. 471.

22. Harry Golden, *Mr. Kennedy and the Negro* (Cleveland, 1964), p. 32.
23. Margaret Laing, *The Next Kennedy* (New York, 1968), pp. 191-192. See also Nick Thimmesch and William Johnson, *Robert Kennedy at 40* (New York, 1965), p. 89, and Schlesinger, *A Thousand Days,* p. 930.
24. Golden, *Mr. Kennedy and the Negro,* p. 32.
25. Schlesinger, *A Thousand Days,* pp. 930-931.
26. See Fleming, "The Federal Executive and Civil Rights: 1961-1965," pp. 922-923.

## Notes for Chapter 3

1. See Schlesinger, *A Thousand Days,* p. 933, and also Marvin Weisbord, "Civil Rights on the New Frontier," *Progressive,* 26 (January 1962), 16.
2. Fleming, "The Federal Executive and Civil Rights: 1961-1965," p. 926.
3. Ibid.
4. *Executive Support of Civil Rights* (Atlanta, 1962), p. 25.
5. Schlesinger, *A Thousand Days,* p. 932.
6. *Kennedy,* p. 477.
7. *A Thousand Days,* p. 932, and *Kennedy,* p. 477.
8. *A Thousand Days,* p. 936, and *Kennedy,* p. 478.
9. Donald B. King and Charles W. Quick, eds., *Legal Aspects of the Civil Rights Movement* (Detroit, 1965), p. 109.
10. Ibid.
11. Letter from Dean Rusk to Robert Kennedy dated May 29, 1961, Department of State *Bulletin,* 44 (June 19, 1961), 976.
12. King and Quick, *Legal Aspects of the Civil Rights Movement,* p. 113.
13. United States Commission of Civil Rights, *Freedom to the Free* (Washington, 1963), p. 138.
14. Benjamin Muse, *Ten Years of Prelude: The Story of Integra-*

*tion Since the Supreme Court's 1954 Decision* (New York, 1964), p. 208.

15. Robert C. Dixon, Jr., "Civil Rights and Transportation and the ICC," *George Washington Law Review,* 31 (October 1962), 227.

16. Bickel, *Politics and the Warren Court,* p. 58; King and Quick, *Legal Aspects of the Civil Rights Movement,* pp. 113-114; and *Executive Support of Civil Rights,* p. 14.

17. King and Quick, *Legal Aspects of the Civil Rights Movement,* p. 125.

18. Robert G. Dixon, Jr., "Civil Rights in Air Transportation and Government Initiative," *Virginia Law Review,* 49 (March 1963), 225-228, and Bickel, *Politics and the Warren Court,* p. 58.

19. Anthony Lewis et al., *Portrait of a Decade: The Second American Revolution* (New York, 1964), pp. 117-118.

20. *Revolution in Civil Rights* (Washington, 1967), p. 49.

21. Sorensen, *Kennedy,* pp. 264-265.

22. Allan Nevins, ed., *President John F. Kennedy: The Burden and the Glory* (New York, 1964), pp. 170-171. See also John P. Roche, *The Quest for a Dream: The Development of Civil Rights and Human Relations* (New York, 1963), p. 258.

23. *Freedom to the Free,* p. 142. For the full text see Executive Order 11063, November 20, 1962, *Federal Register,* 27 (1962), 11527-11530. See also Monroe Berger, *Equality by Statute: The Revolution in Civil Rights* (New York, 1967), p. 42.

24. Harold C. Fleming, "Civil Rights," *Britannica Book of the Year: 1963* (Chicago, 1963), p. 277.

25. Sorensen, *Kennedy,* pp. 264-265.

26. *Freedom to the Free,* p. 141.

27. Fleming, "The Federal Executive and Civil Rights: 1961-1965," p. 931. For a good discussion of actions by federal agencies in the next few months after the housing order was issued, see Berl I. Bernhard, "Civil Rights

After Five Years," *North Carolina Law Review,* 42 (December 1963), 50-66.

28. "The Pentagon Jumps into the Race Relations Fight," *U. S. News & World Report,* 55 (August 19, 1963), 49. See also *Civil Rights '63* (Washington, 1963), pp. 193-194.

29. Stillman, *Integration of the Negro in the Armed Forces,* p. 115.

30. Letter from President Kennedy to Gerhard A. Gesell dated June 22, 1962, *Public Papers of the President, John F. Kennedy, 1962* (Washington, 1963), p. 508.

31. The President's Committee on Equal Opportrnity in the Armed Forces—Initial Report, "Equality of Treatment and Opportunity for Negro Military Personnel Stationed Within the United States," *Congressional Record,* 109, Pt. 9, 14359.

32. Ibid., p. 14360.

33. Ibid., p. 14367.

34. Ibid.

35. Letter from President Kennedy to Robert McNamara dated June 21, 1963, *Public Papers of the Presidents: John F. Kennedy, 1963* (Washington, 1964), p. 496.

36. Defense Department Memorandum, July 26, 1963, *Congressional Record,* 109, Pt. 2, 14358-14359.

37. "The Pentagon Jumps into the Race Relations Fight," p. 50, and "Georgia's Vinson: Battling the Pentagon, *U. S. News & World Report,* 55 (September 30, 1963), 16.

38. "Civil Rights: The Kennedy Record," p. 12. The Southern Regional Council report stated that nine cases had been filed by the previous administration, and three were completed *(Executive Support of Civil Rights,* p. 11).

39. Sorensen, *Kennedy,* p. 479.

40. Thimmesch and Johnson, *Robert Kennedy at 40,* p. 98.

41. *Congressional Quarterly Almanac 1962,* (Washington, 1962), pp. 371-375, and Berl I. Bernhard, "The Federal Fact-Finding Experience—A Guide to Negro Enfranchisement," *Law and Contemporary Problems,* 27 (Summer 1962), 479.

42. *Congressional Quarterly Almanac 1962*, pp. 404-406.
43. Lewis, *Portrait of a Decade*, p. 117, and Fleming, *Britannica Book of the Year 1963*, p. 275.
44. *Freedom to the Free*, p. 198.
45. Muse, *Ten Years of Prelude*, p. 240, and Fleming, *Britannica Book of the Year 1963*, p. 275.
46. Fleming, "The Federal Executive and Civil Rights: 1961-1965," p. 938.
47. *Congressional Quarterly Almanac, 1963*, p. 339.
48. Sorensen, *Kennedy*, p. 479.
49. Lewis, *Portrait of a Decade*, p. 119, and Fleming, "The Federal Executive and Civil Rights," p. 940.
50. Sorensen, *Kennedy*, p. 480; Lewis, *Portrait of a Decade*, p. 119; Laing, *The Next Kennedy*, p. 193; and Thimmesch and Johnson, *Robert Kennedy at 40*, p. 93.
51. Steamer, "Presidential Stimulus and School Desegregation," p. 31.
52. Ibid.
53. Sorensen, *Kennedy*, p. 264; *Freedom to the Free*, p. 159; and Muse, *Ten Years of Prelude*, p. 241.
54. King and Quick, *Legal Aspects of the Civil Rights Movement*, p. 263, and *Freedom to the Free*, p. 160.
55. *Freedom to the Free*, p. 159.
56. "Administration Desegregation Acts Bring Controversy," *Congressional Quarterly Weekly Report*, 20 (August 3, 1962), 1295.
57. Ibid.
58. See James W. Silver, *Mississippi: The Closed Society* (New York, 1964), for the viewpoint of one academician who was present.
59. Russell H. Barrett, *Integration at Ole Miss* (Chicago, 1965), pp. 93-94. Barrett was another academician who was present.
60. Evelyn Lincoln, *My Twelve Years with John F. Kennedy* (New York, 1965), pp. 315-316; Silver, *Mississippi: The Closed Society*, p. vii; and Barrett, *Integration at Ole Miss*, pp. 221-222.

61. Radio and Television Address to the American People on Civil Rights, *Public Papers of the Presidents: John F. Kennedy, 1963* (Washington, 1964), p. 469.
62. Harold C. Fleming, "Civil Rights," *Britannica Book of the Year 1964* (Chicago, 1964), p. 258. See Lewis, *Portrait of a Decade,* p. 119, for slightly different figures.
63. Fleming, *Britannica Book of the Year 1964,* p. 258, and *Public Papers of the Presidents: John F. Kennedy, 1963,* p. 662.
64. Steamer, "Presidential Stimulus and School Desegregation," pp. 31-32.
65. *Public Papers of the Presidents: John F. Kennedy, 1961* (Washington, 1962), p. 150. For the full text see Executive Order 10925, March 6, 1961, *Federal Register,* 26 (1961), 1977-1979.
66. *Executive Support of Civil Rights,* p. 32, and *Report to the President by the President's Committee on Equal Employment Opportunity* (Washington, 1963), p. 3.
67. *Executive Support of Civil Rights,* p. 32.
68. Birnbaum, "Equal Employment and Executive Order 10925," pp. 31-32.
69. *Report to the President. . . ,* p. 34.
70. Ibid., p. 35.
71. Alan B. Batchelder, "Economic Forces Serving the Ends of Negro Protest," *Annals of the American Academy of Political and Social Science,* 37 (January 1965), 86.
72. *Freedom to the Free,* p. 131.
73. *Report to the President. . . ,* p. 108.
74. Ibid.
75. Ibid., p. 115.
76. Ibid., p. 118.
77. Theodore Leskes, "The Civil Rights Story: A Year's Review," *Wayne Law Review,* 9 (Spring 1963), 510.
78. "Integration: 100 Years Later," *Newsweek,* 61 (February 25, 1963), 27. See also Herbert Hill, "Racial Inequality in Employment: The Patterns of Discrimination," *Annals of the American Academy of Political and Social Science,* 37 (January 1965), 33.

79. "Integration: 100 Years Later," p. 27.
80. Berl I. Bernhard, "Civil Rights After Five Years," *North Carolina* Law Review, 42 (December 1963), 61. See also Executive Order 11114 in *Report to the President. . .*, pp. 140-141.
81. Fleming, *Britannica Book of the Year 1964*, p 261.
82. Fleming, "The Federal Executive and Civil Rights," p. 934. In 1961 the Civil Rights Commission expressed skepticism about the effectiveness of the President's Executive Order 10925 (Foster Rhea Dulles, *The Civil Rights Commission. 1957-1965*, Lansing, Mich., 1968, pp. 141-142.)
83. Fleming, "The Federal Executive and Civil Rights," p. 934.
84. Sorensen, *Kennedy*, p. 747.

## Notes for Chapter 4

1. Bickel, *Politics and the Warren Court*, p. 57.
2. *Congressional Quarterly Almanac 1963*, p. 671.
3. *Public Papers of the Presidents: John F. Kennedy, 1963*, p. 14.
4. Ibid., p. 222.
5. Ibid., pp. 222-224.
6. Ibid., pp. 225-227.
7. Dulles, *The Civil Rights Commission*, pp. 183-184.
8. "Integration: Angry Language," *Newsweek*, 61 (April 29, 1968), p. 145.
9. Dulles, *The Civil Righs Commission*, p. 187.
10. Lerone Bennett, Jr., *What Manner of Man: A Biography of Martin Luther King, Jr.* (Chicago, 1964), p. 164, and Schlesinger, *A Thousand Days*, p. 959.
11. William Robert Miller, *Martin Luther King, Jr.* (New York, 1968), p. 15.
12. *Public Papers of the Presidents: John F. Kennedy, 1963*, p. 372.
13. Ibid., pp. 397-398.

14. Telegram to Governor Wallace, May 13, 1963, ibid., p. 182.
15. Sorensen, *Kennedy,* p. 489. See also Schlesinger, *A Thousand Days,* p. 960.
16. Schlesinger, *A Thousand Days,* p. 959.
17. Laing, *The Next Kennedy,* p. 201.
18. Sorensen, *Kennedy,* p. 492.
19. Ibid., p. 494.
20. *Public Papers of the Presidents: John F. Kennedy, 1963,* p. 469.
21. Ibid., p. 470.
22. The author refers to the president's efforts to reduce the risk of a nuclear war.
23. "Kennedy in the Presidency: A Premature Appraisal," *Political Science Quarterly,* 79 (1964), 325-326.
24. *The Southern Mystique* (New York, 1964), p. 237.
25. Sundquist, *Politics and Policy,* p. 263.
26. Special Message to the Congress on Civil Rights and Job Opportunities, *Public Papers of the Presidents: John F. Kennedy, 1963,* p. 484.
27. Ibid., pp. 484-485.
28. Sorensen, *Kennedy,* p. 501; Bennett, *What Manner of Man,* p. 157; "Kennedy Submits the Civil Rights Bill to Congress," *Congressional Quarterly Weekly Report,* 21 (June 21, 1963), 1000; and Fleming, "The Federal Executive and Civil Rights," p. 943.
29. Sundquist, *Politics and Policy,* p. 264.
30. Sorensen, *Kennedy,* p. 502.
31. "Civil Rights Revolt," *New Republic,* 149 (November 2, 1963), 4, and "Kennedy's on the Spot," *Economist,* 209 (October 26, 1963), 374-375.
32. *New York Times,* October 17, 1963, p. 1.
33. "Civil Rights Bill," *Congressional Quarterly Weekly Report,* 21 (October 18, 1963), p. 1814.
34. Sorensen, *Kennedy,* p. 501; Schlesinger, *A Thousand Days,* pp. 972-973; and Louis W. Koenig, *Official Makers of Public Policy: Congress and the President* (Greenview, Ill., 1965), p. 136. See also *New York Times,* October

23-30, 1963, passim, and "Halleck and McCulloch," *Newsweek*, 62 (November 11, 1963), 34.

35. Sundquist, *Politics and Policy,* pp. 264-265; *Congressional Quarterly Almanac 1963,* pp. 349-351; and *Revolution in Civil Rights,* p. 50.

36. Sundquist, *Politics and Policy,* p. 265. See also Bickel, *Politics and the Warren Court,* p. 119, and Burke Marshall, *Federalism and Civil Rights* (New York, 1964), pp. 38-39.

38. *Public Papers of the Presidents: John F. Kennedy, 1963,* p. 820.

39. *Congressional Quarterly Almanac 1963,* p. 351.

40. Samuel Lubell, *White and Black: Test of a Nation* (New York, 1964), pp. 7-8; Sorensen, *Kennedy,* p. 505; Benjamin Muse, *The American Negro Revolution* (Bloomington, 1968), p. 84; Schlesinger, *A Thousand Days,* p. 968 and "Is JFK Weaker Politically?" *U. S. News & World Report,* 55 (November 18, 1963), 43-46.

# Selected Bibliography

## Government Documents

*Civil Rights '63. Report of the United States Commission on Civil Rights.* Washington, D.C.: U.S. Government Printing Office, September 1963.

*Congressional Record,* 109, Pt. 11, 88th Cong., 1st Sess., 1963.

Department of State *Bulletin,* 44 (June 19, 1961).

*Federal Register,* 26 (1961) and 27 (1962).

*Public Papers of the Presidents: John F. Kennedy,* 1961-1963. 3 vols. Washington, D.C.: U.S. Government Printing Office, 1962-1964.

*Report to the President by the President's Committee on Equal Employment Opportunity.* Washington, D.C.: U.S. Government Printing Office, 1963.

U.S. Commission on Civil Rights. *Freedom to the Free.* Washington, D.C.: U.S. Government Printing Office, 1963.

## Books

Barrett, Russell H., *Integration at Ole Miss.* Chicago: Quadrangle Books, 1965.

Bennett, Lerone, Jr. *What Manner of Man: A Biography of Martin Luther King, Jr.* Chicago: Johnson Publishing Co., 1964.

Berger, Monroe. *Equality by Statue: The Revolution in Civil Rights.* Garden City, N.Y.: Doubleday & Co., Inc., 1967.

82

Bickel, Alexander M. *Politics and the Warren Court.* New York: Harper & Row, 1965.

*Congressional Quarterly Almanac 1962.* Washington, D.C.: Congressional Quarterly Service, 1962.

——————— 1963. Washington, D.C.: Congressional Quarterly Service, 1963.

Dulles, Foster Rhea. *The Civil Rights Commission: 1957-1965.* Lansing: Michigan State University Press, 1968.

Eisenhower, Dwight D. *The White House Years: Waging Peace 1956-1961.* Garden City, N.Y.: Doubleday & Co., Inc., 1965.

Fleming, Harold C. "Civil Rights," *Britannica Book of the Year 1963.* Chicago: Encyclopedia Britannica, Inc., 1963.

———————. "Civil Rights," *Britannica Book of the Year 1964.* Chicago: Encyclopedia Britannica, Inc., 1964.

Golden, Harry. *Mr. Kennedy and the Negro.* Cleveland: The World Publishing Co., 1964.

Hughes, Emmet John. *The Ordeal of Power: A Political Memoir of the Eisenhower Years.* New York: Atheneum Publishers, Inc., 1963.

King, Donald B., and Charles W. Quick (eds.). *Legal Aspects of the Civil Rights Movement.* Detroit: Wayne State Univesity Press, 1965.

Koenig, Louis W. *The Chief Executive.* New York: Harcourt, Brace & World, 1964.

———————. *Official Makers of Public Policy. Congress and the President.* Glenville, Ill.: Scott, Foresman and Co., 1965.

Laing, Margaret. *The Next Kennedy.* New York: Coward-McCann, Inc., 1968.

Lincoln, Evelyn. *My Twelve Years with John F. Kennedy.* New York: David McKay Co., Inc., 1965.

Lewis, Anthony, et al. *Portrait of a Decade: The Second American Revolution.* New York: Random House, 1964.

Lubell, Samuel. *White and Black: Test of a Nation.* New York: Harper & Row, 1964.

Marshall, Burke. *Federalism and Civil Rights.* New York: Columbia University Press, 1964.

Miller, William Robert. *Martin Luther King, Jr.: His Life, Martyr-dom and Meaning for the World.* New York: Weybright and Talley, 1968.

Muse, Benjamin. *Ten Years of Prelude: The Story of Integration Since the Supreme Court's 1954 Decision.* New York Viking Press, 1964.

—————. *The American Revolution: From Non-Violence to Black Power 1963-1967.* Bloomington: Indiana University Press, 1968.

Nevins, Allan, ed. *President John F. Kennedy: The Burden and the Glory.* New York: Harper & Row, 1964.

Roche, John P. *The Quest for a Dream: The Development of Civil Rights and Human Relations.* New York: The Macmillan Co., 1963.

Schlesinger, Arthur M., Jr. *A Thousand Days. John F. Kennedy in the White House.* Boston: Houghton Mifflin Co., 1965.

Silver, James W. *Mississippi: The Closed Society.* New York: Harcourt, Brace & World, 1964.

Sorensen, Theodore C. *Kennedy.* New York: Harper & Row, 1965.

Stillman, Richard J., II. *Integration of the Negro in the Armed Forces.* New York: Frederick A. Praeger, 1968.

Sundquist, James L. *Politics and Policy: The Eisenhower, Kennedy and Johnson Years.* Washington, D.C.: The Brookings Institution, 1968.

Thimmesch, Nick, and William Johnson. *Robert Kennedy at 40.* New York: W. W. Norton & Co., 1965.

White, Theodore H. *The Making of the President 1960.* New York: Atheneum Publishers, Inc., 1962.

Zinn, Howard. *The Southern Mystique.* New York: Alfred A. Knopf, 1964.

## Periodicals

"Administration Desegregation Acts Bring Controversy." *Congressional Quarterly Weekly Report,* 20 (August 3, 1962), 1294-1299.

Batchelder, Alan B. "Economic Forces Serving the Ends of Negro Protest." *Annals of the American Academy of Political and Social Science,* 357 (January 1965), 80-88.

Bernard, Berl I. "The Federal Fact-Finding Experience—A Guide to Negro Enfranchisement." *Law and Contemporary Problems,* 27 (Summer 1962), 468-480.

——————. "Civil Rights After Five Years." *North Carolina Law Review,* 42 (December 1963), 50-66.

Bickel, Alexander M. "Civil Rights: The Kennedy Record." *New Republic,* 147 (December 15, 1962), 11-16.

"Bipartisan Civil Rights Approved." *Congressional Quarterly Weekly Report,* 21 (November 1, 1963), 1875-1880.

Birnbaum, Owen. "Equal Employment Opportunity and Executive Order 10925." *University of Kansas Law Review,* 11 (October, 1962), 17-34.

"Civil Rights." *Congressional Quarterly Weekly Report,* 18 (August 12, 1960), 1434-1435.

"Civil Rights Bill." *Congressional Quarterly Weekly Report,* 21 (October 18, 1963), 1814.

"Civil Rights Planks in the Party Platforms." *Current History,* 39 (October 1960), 237-240, 244.

"Civil Rights Pledges Trouble Kennedy Administration." *Congressional Quarterly Weekly Report,* 19 (April 21, 1961), 667-668.

"Civil Rights Revolt." *New Republic,* 149 (November 2, 1963), 4-5.

*Congressional Digest,* 39 (October, 1960), 253, 255.

Dixon, Robert G. "Civil Rights and Transportation and the ICC." *George Washington Law Review,* 31 (October, 1962), 198-241.

——————. "Civil Rights in Air Transportation and Government Initiative." *Virginia Law Review,* 49 (March 1963), 205-231.

Fleming, Harold C. "The Federal Executive and Civil Rights: 1961-1965." *Daedalus.* 94 (Fall 1965), 921-948.

"Georgia's Vinson Battling the Pentagon." *News & World Report,* 55 (September 30, 1963), 16.

"Halleck and McCulloch." *Newsweek,* 62 (November 11, 1963), 34-37.

Hill, Herbert. "Racial Inequality in Employment: The Patterns of Discrimination." *The Annals of the American Academy of Political and Social Science,* 357 (January 1965), 30-47.

"Integration: Angry Language," *Newsweek,* 61 (April 29, 1963), 25-26.

"Integration: 100 Years Later." *Newsweek,* 61 (February 25, 1963), 26-27.

"Is JFK Weaker Politically?" *U.S. News & World Report,* 55 (November 18, 1963), 43-46.

"Kennedy's on the Spot.' *The Economist,* 209 (October 26, 1963), 374-375.

"Kennedy Submits the Civil Rights Bill to Congress." *Congressional Quarterly Weekly Report,* 21 (June 21, 1963), 997-1000.

King, Martin Luther, Jr. "Equal Now." *Nation,* 192 (February 4, 1961), 91-95.

Leskes, Theodore. "The Civil Rights Story: A Year's Review." *Wayne Law Review,* 9 (Spring 1963), 484-512.

Lytle, Clifford M. "The History of the Civil Rights Bill of 1964." *Journal of Negro History,* 51 (October 1966), 275-296.

Neustadt, Richard E. "Kennedy in the Presidency: A Premature Appraisal." *Political Science Quarterly,* 79 (September, 1964), 321-334.

"Nixon: The Goals of a New Administration." *U.S. News & World Report,* 49 (August 8, 1960), 94-99.

"The Pentagon Jumps into the Fight." *U.S. News & World Report,* 55 (August 19, 1963), 49-50.

Weisbord, Marvin. "Civil Rights on the New Frontiers." *Progressive,* 26 (January 1962), 15-19.

## Pamphlets

*Executive Support of Civil Rights.* Atlanta: Southern Regional Council, March 13, 1962.

*Federal Executive and Civil Rights, The.* Atlanta: Southern Regional Council, January, 1961.


Newspapers

*New York Times,* 1960-1963.